RORSCHACHIANA XIX

RORSCHACHIANA
XIX

Yearbook of the
International Rorschach Society

Edited by

Irving B. Weiner
University of South Florida Psychiatry Center, Tampa, FL

Hogrefe & Huber Publishers
Seattle · Toronto · Bern · Göttingen

© Copyright 1994 by Hogrefe & Huber Publishers

ISSN 1192-5604

ISBN 0-88937-128-8
Hogrefe & Huber Publishers · Seattle · Toronto · Bern · Göttingen
ISBN 3-456-82501-3
Hogrefe & Huber Publishers · Bern · Göttingen · Seattle · Toronto

Printed in Germany

Table of Contents

Addresses of First Authors

Dr. Irving B. Weiner
University of South Florida
Psychiatry Center
3515 East Fletcher Avenue
Tampa, FL 33613
USA

Dr. John E. Exner, Jr.
Rorschach Workshops
P. O. Box 9010
Asheville, NC 28815
USA

Prof. Danilo Silva
Faculty of Psychology
University of Lisbon
Calcada dos Mestres, 96, 30
1000 Lisbon
Portugal

Prof. Concepcion Sendin
Hospital de Leganes
Francisco de Vitoria
E-28007 Madrid
Spain

Dr. Bruce Lazar Smith
2515 Milvia Street,
Suite D
Berkeley, CA 94704
USA

Prof. Leonid F. Burlatchuk
Vanvarskogo Vosstaniya, 3 ap. 161
252010 Kiev
Ukraine

Prof. Françoise Brelet-Foulard
Université Paris XIII
Avenue Jean-Baptiste Clement
F-93430 Villetaneuse
France

Prof. Helena Lunazzi de Jubany
Universidad Nacional de La Plata
Calle 54 No. 456-90 Piso, Dpto. 1
1900 La Plata, RA
Argentina

Dr. Marvin W. Acklin
850 West Hind Avenue, Suite 209
Honolulu, HI 96821
USA

Prof. Matilde Raez de Ramirez
Pontificia Universidad Catolica
Av. Prescott 330 (San Isidro)
Lima 27
Peru

Mr. Harald Janson
Department of Psychology
University of Stockholm
S-10691 Stockholm
Sweden

Speaking Rorschach:
Building Bridges of Understanding

Irving B. Weiner

University of South Florida, Tampa, FL, USA

One year ago it was my privilege to write an editor's introduction to the first issue of *Rorschachiana* being published as the annual *Yearbook of the International Rorschach Society*. I observed that increasing communication among Rorschach clinicians and researchers around the world was breaking down previous barriers to our learning from each other, and I concluded that being able to speak Rorschach means having command of an international language.

In addition to expanding our knowledge, increased communication is building new bridges of understanding between diverse approaches" to the interpretation of the Rorschach Inkblot Method. Over the years, there have been two major approaches to using the Rorschach. One is a perceptual approach that focuses primarily on using subjects' cognitive structuring of the inkblots as a source of information about their personality style. The other is an associational approach that focuses primarily on using subject's thematic imagery in response to the inkblots as a source of information about their personality dynamics.

At times the perceptual and associational approaches to Rorschach have been characterized, respectively, as the "empirical approach" and the "psychoanalytic approach." However, this characterization is misleading. Psychoanalytic theory has long been concerned with personality structure as well as personality dynamics, and empiricists can be as interested in quantifying aspects of Rorschach content as Rorschach structure. Nevertheless, there clearly has been a divergence among Rorschachers who prefer to base their interpretations primarily on structural variables and those who attend primarily to content elaborations. It is probably fair to say that, for many people entering the field, opting for a structural preference or a content preference has been a way of establishing their identity as a Rorschach clinician or researcher—and perhaps also, it must be said, has been a basis for ignoring or disparaging the work of Rorschachers with a preference different from theirs.

More and more in present times, however, we are listening as well as talking to each other. We recognize that Bohm (1951/1958), a strict structurist in the tradition of Hermann Rorschach, proposed such psychodynamic content interpretations as taking the response of "Two men want to shake hands or are drawing back" as evidence of "tendencies toward flight or splitting" (p. 115). We recall that Rapaport, perhaps our most distinguished psychoanalytic Rorschach theorist, insisted that Rorschach responses involve both perceptual and associational processes: "One must never neglect the integration of the two processes ... It would not be correct to reason that the Rorschach response is to be considered mainly either a perceptual product of one of free association" (Rapaport, Gill, & Schafer, 1946/1968, pp. 174 & 276).

We appreciate that the Comprehensive System, which began as an almost exclusively structural approach to the Rorschach, has been modified to incorporate systematic attention to thematic imagery (Exner, 1993). We are aware that contemporary advances in psychoanalytic object relations perspectives on the Rorschach involve careful codification of content themes (Lerner, 1993; Stricker & Healey, 1990).

At the XIVth Congress of the International Rorschach Society in Lisbon in July of 1993, the content of the presentations bore witness to a new era of constructive integration among different approaches to the Rorschach Inkblot Method and mutual respect among proponents of different ways of using the instrument. Of equal importance, the personal and social interactions of participants in the Congress bore witness to a new era of good feeling and camaraderie among Rorschachers of different persuasions and from different parts of the world.

And so we continue in this second issue of the *Rorschach Yearbook* with diverse contributions concerning issues of research and practice, reflecting various theoretical points of view, and prepared by colleagues from many countries—Argentina, France, Peru, Portugal, Spain, Sweden, the Ukraine, and the United States.

Résumé

Il y a de ça un an, j'ai eu le privilège, en ma qualité de Rédacteuren Chef, de rédiger l'introduction au premier numéro de *Rorschachiana* devenu la publication annuelle de la Société Internationale du Rorschach, sous le titre de *Yearbook of the International Rorschach Society*. Je constatai alors qu'un accroissement de communication entre praticiens et chercheurs à travers le monde était en train de battre en brèche d'anciennes barrières qui nous avaient empêchés de nous écouter mutuellement et d'apprendre les uns des autres. J'en avais conclu que parler Rorschach nécessitait de passer par un langage international.

En plus d'accroître nos connaissances, la communication qui se développe aujourd'hui jette de nouveaux ponts entre différentes approches dans l'interprétation de la Méthode des taches d'encre de Rorschach. On a connu deux perspectives majeures. L'une d'elle est une approche perceptive qui se centre essentiellement sur l'analyse de la manière dont le sujet structure les planches pour décrire des styles de personnalité. L'autre est une approche associationniste qui se centre essentiellement sur la thématique de la réponse pour décrire la dynamique de la personnalité.

On a généralement caractérisé ces approches comme étant respectivement "empirique" et "psychanalytique," mais ces étiquettes semblent réductrices. La théorie psychanalytique s'intéresse depuis bien longtemps tout autant à la structure qu'aux aspects dynamiques de la personnalité, et les empiristes peuvent montrer tout autant d'intérêt pour la quantification des éléments du contenu que pour la structure Rorschach. Et pourtant, on ne peut nier la réelle divergence qui a existé entre les tenants d'une interprétation basée avant tout sur les variables structurales et les tenants d'une interprétation tournée vers l'analyse des contenus. On pourrait même dire que, pour beaucoup de personnes entrant dans la profession, opter pour l'analyse structurale ou pour l'analyse de contenus a été un moyen d'établir son identité comme praticien et/ou chercheur dans le domaine du Rorschach. Cette prise de position s'est souvent accompagnée d'un désintérêt, voire d'un mépris, pour les travaux Rorschach de "l'autre bord."

Aujourd'hui, nous commençons à nous écouter les uns les autres, et même à nous parler. Nous savons que Bohm (1951/1958), tenant de l'analyse structurale dans la plus pure tradition d'Herman Rorschach, a pu proposer des interprétations psychodynamiques de contenus, considérant par exemple une réponse telle que "Deux hommes veulent se serrer la main ou bien ils se reculent" comme reflétant "des tendances à la fuite ou au clivage" (p. 115). Nous nous souvenons que Rapaport, l'un des plus grands théoriciens de l'approche psychanalytique du Rorschach, insistait sur le rôle conjoint des processus perceptifs et associatifs: "On ne doit jamais sousestimer l'importance de l'intégration des deux processus ... Il serait erroné de soutenir que la réponse Rorschach est un pur produit de la perception, ou de l'association libre" (Rapaport, Gill, & Schafer, 1946/1968, pp. 174 & 276).

Nous constatons que le Système Intégré, qui a débuté dans une perspective exclusivement structurale, s'est progressivement modifié et qu'il intègre aujourd'hui la dimension thématique (Exner, 1993). Nous sommes conscients que les avancées contemporaines du modèle psychanalytique des relations d'objet dans le champ du Rorschach passent par une codification attentive de la thématique des contenus (Lerner, 1993; Stricker & Healey, 1990).

Au XIVème Congrès de la Société Internationale du Rorschach de juillet 1993 à Lisbonne, le contenu des communications témoignait du développement d'une nouvelle ère d'intégration constructive entre différentes approches de la Méthode Rorschach, et reflétait un respect mutuel entre les différentes écoles. Tout aussi importants furent les échanges personnels et sociaux des participants au Congrès, qui témoignèrent d'une nouvelle ère dans les relations, marquées par des sentiments positifs de camaraderie.

Et c'est ainsi que, dans ce deuxième numéro du *Rorschach Yearbook*, nous retrouvons diverses contributions portant sur des questions de pratique et de recherche en matière de Rorschach, qui reflètent différents points de vue et qui ont été rédigées par des collègues issus de nombreux pays, l'Argentine, l'Espagne, les EtatsUnis, la France, le Pérou, le Portugal, la Suède et l'Ukraine.

Resumen

Hace un año tuve el privilegio de escribir una introcucción editorial al primer número de *Rorschachiana*, publicada como el *Anuario do la Sociedad Rorschach Internacional*. Observaba en ella que el incremento en la communicación entre los clínicos e investigadores del Rorschach alrededor del mundo estaba derrumbando barreras previas a la posibilidad de aprender unos de otros, y conclui que ser capaz de hablar Rorschach significaba dominar un lenguaje internacional.

Además de expandir nuestro conocimiento, el incremento en la communicación está construyendo nuevos puentes de entendimimiento entre diversos enforques para la interpretación del Método Rorschach.

Con el paso de los años, han habido principalmente dos enfoques en el usoe del Rorschach. Uno de ellos es un enfoque perceptivo, el cual se centra fundamentalmente en utilizar la estructuración cognitiva de las manchas de tinta que realizan los sujectos como fuente de información acerca de su estilo de personalidad. El otro es un enfoque asociativo, el cual se centra fundamentalmente en utilizzr las imágenes temáticas del sujeto en respuesta a las manchas de tinta como fuente de información acerca de la dinámica de su personalidad.

En ocasiones, los enfoques perceptivo y asociativo al Rorschach han sido caracterizados como el "enfoque empirico" y el "enfoque psicoanalitico" respectivamente. Sin embargo, esta caracterización se presta a confusiones. La teoría psicoanalitica ha venido preocupándose tanto por la estructura como por la dinámica de la personalidad, y los empiricistas pueden estar tan interesados en cuantificar los aspectos de de estructura como del contenido del Rorschach. De cualquier manera, ha existido una clara divergencia entre los rorschachistas que prefieren basar primariamente sus interpretaciones en las variables estructurales y aquellos que atienden en primer lugar a las elaboraciones del contenido. Probablemente se pueda decir con justeza que, para much gente que se introduce en el campe, optar por preferir lo estructural o el contenido has constituido una forma de establecer la propia identidad como clinico or investigador del Rorschach—y tal vez también, hay que decirlo, ha sido una base para ignorar o descalificar el trabajo de los rorschachistas con une preferencia distinta.

Cada vez más en la actualidad, sin embargo, nos escuchamos y hablamos unos con otros. Reconocemos que Bohm (1951/1958), un partidario estricto de lo estructural en la tradición de Hermann Rorschach, propuso interpretaciones psicodinámicas del contenido, tales como tomar el respuesta: "Dos hombres que quieren darse la mano o están desunión" (p. 115). Recordamos que Rapaport, tal vez nuestro más distinguido teórico psicoanalítico del Rorschach, insistió end que las respuestas involucran tanto procesos perceptivos como asociativos: "o se debe nunca descuidar la integración de ambos procesos ... No seria correcto pensar ques la respuesta al Rorschach deba ser considerada fundamentalmente como un producto perceptivo o como el resultado de la asociación libre" (Rapaport, Gill, & Schafer, 1946/1968, pp. 174 & 276).

Apreciamos que es Sistema Comprehensivo, el caul comenzó como un enfoque exclusivamente estructural, ha sido modificado para incorporar la atención systemática a los temas que las imágenes aportan

5

(Exner, 1993). Estamos conscientes de que los avances contemporáneos en las perspectivas psiconalíticas sobre las relaciones objectales incluyen la codificación cuidadosa de los temas del contenidod (Lerner, 1993; Stricker & Healey, 1990).

En al XIVavo Congreso de la Sociedad Internacional de Rorschach in Lisboa en Julio de 1993, el contenido de las presentaciones testimoniaron une nueva era de integración constructiva entre los diferentes enfoques del Método Rorschach y el respeto mutuo entre los proponentes de diferentes maneras de usar el instrumento. Igualmente importante, las interacciones personales y sociales de los participatnes del Congreso atestiguaron una nueva era de sentimientos positivos y camaradería entre rorschachistas de derentes convicciones y entre aquellos provenientes de diferentes partes del mundo.

De esa manera continuamos en este segundo número del *Anuario Rorschach* con diversas contribuciones acerca de questiones de la investigación y de la práctica, reflejando variados puntos de vista, en trabajos preparados por colegas de muchos paises—Argentina, Francia, Perú, Portugal, España, Suecia, Ucrania, y Estados Unidos.

References

Bohm, E. (1951/1958). *A textbook in Rorschach diagnosis.* New York: Grune & Stratton.

Exner, J. E. (1993). *The Rorschach: A comprehensive system. Vol. 1. Basic processes* (3rd ed.). New York: Wiley.

Lerner, P. M. (1993). Object relations theory and the Rorschach. *Rorschachiana, 18,* 45–57.

Rapaport, D., Gill, M., & Schafer, R. (1946/1968). *Diagnostic psychological testing* (Rev. ed. edited by R. R. Holt). New York: International Universities Press.

Stricker, G., & Healey, B. J. (1990). Projective assessment of object relations: A review of the empirical literature. *Psychological Assessment, 2,* 219–230.

Rorschach and the Study of the Individual

John E. Exner, Jr.

Rorschach Workshops, Asheville, NC, USA

Since the Rorschach was first published 1922, interest in its applications has grown steadily throughout the world. The test continues to be a focus of both theory and research, much of which centers on either of two major issues. The first concerns how the test works, that is, how is it that a relatively few samples of behavior (responses) yield so much information about the subject? The second concerns how the test can be used to differentiate groups of people, that is, what features of one group are idiosyncratic to that group, such a differentiating nonpatients from patients, schizophrenics from depressives, and so on. This latter category of issues is, in part, related to interest in using the test for differential diagnosis. A third area has received less attention. It concerns the fact that the test yields very important data about each subject as a unique person.

When Rorschach began his own research, first in 1911, and later during the period from 1917 to 1921, he tended to focus on the first two issues noted above. It was only near the end of his work that he perceived the test as being a useful way to capture some of the idiography of the subject. In effect, he had stumbled on to a way to study personality and individual differences. The issue of personality and individual differences has not been afforded much consideration in the Rorschach literature in recent years. This is unfortunate because many who use the Rorschach tend to disregard the potential applications of its richness when using the test.

The Rorschach provides a great deal of information about a subject, and obviously, that information can contribute in an indirect way to differential diagnosis. But that is a relatively minor aspect in using the test. The marvel of the Rorschach is the very personal picture of the subject that it offers. In doing so, it tends to emphasize how each person is different than each other person, even though they may be quite similar in some ways. In effect, it *is* a test of individual differences, the yield from which highlights the psychological strengths and weaknesses of each subject. This sort of information is especially important in the clinical situation because it can be used to identify treatment objectives when some state of disarray exists. It is this use of the Rorschach that seems to be neglected most often by those using the test, and that neglect probably limits the quality of treatment offered to those who have been subjects of the test.

Interest in people and their individuality has existed for centuries, but the notion of personality, as a subject for psychological study, is less than 100 years old. The works of Freud had, of course, received considerable attention beginning in the very late 1800s and the theoretical propositions of many neo-Freudians gained also gained much attention during the first two decades of the 20th Century. But, by 1920, no one in psychology had taken serious interest in the study of personality. Had Rorschach lived longer he might have given greater emphasis to the study of the individual, but that might not have been the case because psychology and psychiatry offered no basis from which to imply that such work had importance.

Allport (1937) noted that a movement called the *psychology of personality* gained interest only after 1920, yielding numerous, but conflicting theories and plentiful, but piecemeal research. Freud, and the neo-Freudians, failed to attract those attempting to address the challenge of defining personality, probably because many aspects of their theoretical models presented complex and untestable postulates. Allport certainly can be credited with bringing the issue into sharper focus. He reviewed some 50 definitions or descriptions of personality and neatly drew the composite into a logical conception by defining personality as the, "the dynamic organization, within the individual, of those psychophysical forces that determine his [or her] unique adjustments to his [or her] environment."

In formulating this definition, Allport noted that the uniqueness of each person creates havoc for science in its search for ways to account for the uniformity of behaviors. He put forth a very compelling challenge; namely, that psychology can only achieve its true purpose when it can deal with the issue of individuality. Allport also offered a strong caution about research orientations that might tend to dismember the total person in ways that would present only fragments of information about whole people, and then attempt to extend that information in ways that would neglect individual differences.

8

Shortly after Allport's classic book *Personality* was released, Henry Murray (1938) published another classic, *Explorations in Personality*. Murray did not attempt to define personality as Allport had done. Instead, he approached the issue of individuality from a different direction. He highlighted it by explicating the unique and sensitive integration of various characteristics within each person. To do so, he neatly illustrated how information, derived from many sources, including psychological tests, could be used to develop a very special picture of a person. Both Murray and Allport strived to distinguish between the idiographic and nomothetic approaches to the study of people. Each, in his own way, argued for an integration of both, that is, an approach which would not simply judge a person against others, but one that would contrast the unique features within one person against those found in others.

The arguments put forth by Allport and Murray stimulated much thinking about the objectives of the psychological study of people and, in effect, created a challenge to those interested in testing (or assessment). Subsequently, the idea of assessing personality and/or psychopathology began to capture much more interest of psychologists than had been the case previously. Although the practice of psychological assessment in the United States usually is dated to 1896 and can be traced earlier in Europe, most attempts to use tests to understand people did not include much personality testing. People calling themselves psychologists did considerable testing, but their efforts focused mainly on issues of intelligence, aptitude, achievement, interest, and so on, and the term *personality* was often used interchangably with psychopathology. A few attempted to devise methods to detect psychopathology during World War I, and some of those efforts did persist into the 1920s and 1930s, with the development of inventories designed to measure some trait-like features such as introversion, extraversion, neuroticism, and the like, but none were used extensively in the clinical setting. Issues of individuality typically were addressed by using data frawn from histories and interviews.

The interest in understanding people as individuals, as purported by Allport and Murray, increased notably during the late 1930s, partly because of the existence of the Rorschach, and mushroomed at an almost incredible pace during World War II with the huge expansion of clinical services provided by the military in several countries, and by the Veterans Administration in the United States. Concurrently, the clinical test battery approach became purported by many, but probably was best articulated by the Rapaport group at the Menninger Foundation during

9

the mid 1940s, leading to the procedure that routinely became called psychodiagnosis.

The objective of psychodiagnosis involved much more than searching out a diagnostic label. It was a multi-test procedure designed to study the person as a unique entity. Implicit to the process was the premise that information about the subject concerning assets, liabilities, conflicts, and so on, would contribute in some significant way to the therapeutic well being of the subject. In other words, the findings contributed to a treatment plan. The notion underlying psychodiagnosis has always been that people behave in ways that are organized and recognizable. That is the basic tenet on which all of psychology is founded. Thus, the objective of the psychodiagnostic procedure was to detect those elements, within the individual, that routinely promoted various behaviors, including the presenting symptoms.

Throughout the 1940s and 1950s, clinical psychologists throughout the world became well recognized and highly regarded for their psycho-diagnostic expertise and the input that they made about patients when issues of diagnosis and/or treatment were discussed. Unfortunately, those interested in the study of personality gradually began to take either of two positions. One, more empirically oriented, argued for the study of personality traits and their relationship to behavior. The second group agreed with many of the basic concepts of trait theorists, but also strongly argued that characterization of traits could not simply be defined in terms of their presence or absence. They preferred to think of personality as a unitary entity and argued that a trait is a descriptive, non-explanatory concept which, following from Allport and Murray, must be weighed in terms of its strength or importance within the individual. Conversely, those arguing for the study of traits maintained that, through the study of individual characteristics, the unitary personality might ultimately evolve, but that more importantly, the approach would be clearly empirical. This approach probably is best illustrated in England, where the work of Eysenck and his group have dominated the assessment picture during the past two decades.

The disagreement about how best to approach issues of personality and individual differences was made more complex beginning in the early 1950's, when a falling out occurred between those who argued strongly in favor of a so-called objective testing approach, and a second group which became closely aligned with what was known as the projective psychology movement. The former argued for a more nomothetic approach to the study of personality, while the latter defined itself as more oriented toward understanding the unique individual. No one profited from that schism, and it was not uncommon in those days for advocates from one group to avoid advocates from the other. In other words, the emphasis on psychodiagnosis, or personality assessment as it began to be called, did persist, but with far less uniformity than had been the case previously.

During the late 1950s another force became prominent among some practicing in clinical psychology in the United States, and has gradually spread to other areas of the world, especially Europe. It is radical behaviorism, which brings with it the notion of the black box, and the message that there is no such thing as personality, or even if there is, it can not be measured through psychological testing. This movement has created a new group of psychologists who have not only avoided personality assessment, but who have campaigned very actively against it, favoring instead the tactics of observation and counting critical incidents as ways of determining targets for intervention. Thus, by the early 1960s in the United States and by the mid-1970s in Europe and some other parts of the world, the once reasonably homogeneous specialty of personality assessment had fragmented considerably.

This divergence probably had its greatest impact in the United States during the mid 1960s and through most of the 1970s as training programs in clinical psychology changed considerably. Students often objected to the laborious time required to learn about test batteries and their applications, and their objections were often reinforced by many in the academic community, from both clinical and non-clinical faculties who voiced opinions that the specialty of psychodiagnosis, or personalty assessment, had only limited value. As curricula changes occurred, many included a marked reduction in the emphasis on that segment of training that had focused on personality assessment and particularly the segment involving the Rorschach and projective methods.

It is sad to note that, in the United States during the 1970s and early 1980s, these altered programs produced huge numbers of graduates who knew little about assessment, less about personality and individual differences, and yet tended to glory in their newly learned therapeutic expertise. The assumption was that personality tests, such as the Rorschach, could not measure the structural features of personality, if they exist, in reliable and valid ways that truly evaluate their full weight in different situations.

These changes did not necessarily lead to less personality testing. In fact, several studies published in the 1980s indicate that the use of psy-

11

chological testing remained at almost the same level in the United States during this controversial period. Unfortunately, those data may simply reflect the fact that psychological testing had become ingrained as a part of many of the routine procedures used with patients, especially in-patients. It is also sad to note that many clinicians continued to use assessment routines that had become little more than a byproduct of intellectual laziness. These are routines that hark back to the days when patients were subject to hours and hours of testing and interviewing, and clinicians took many days to write lengthy reports that often neglected much of the data that they had collected. But the main force that led to a reduction of training and emphasis on personality assessment procedures clearly came from the increased emphasis on therapeutic training and the variety of therapeutic methods that might be employed in different situations.

The reduced interest in personality testing and the study of individual differences has probably increased because an element outside of psychology. It involves the important changes that have been ongoing in psychiatry throughout the world. Beginning in the late 1960s or early 1970s training programs in psychiatry reduced emphasis on the tactics of individual therapy, and extended the emphasis on pharmacological issues as a basis for, or adjunct to intervention. As psychiatry has gradually changed in its emphasis, clinical psychology often paused from its own search for identity to condemn this so called medical model.

The medical model, of course, is strongly embedded in the DSM and WHO manuals that search out a listing of characteristics or traits that are determined to be equivalent within a particular syndrome or diagnosis. Thus, many in contemporary psychiatry now tend to perceive the role of the psychologist as being more competitive, and the procedures of assessment as being of little use unless they contribute to some DSM or WHO designation. They are seemingly unaware of the potential for describing the patient as a unique entity in a way that will contribute to the ultimate well being of the patient. Unfortunately, a lengthy period has ensued in which psychologists have neglected the opportunities to educate colleagues from psychiatry concerning their potential assessment skills, and the way in which those skills can contribute to more precise treatment planning. But even in the area of personality assessment, many of the issues of science have been cast aside. A notable decline has occurred in the area of basic research concerning personality and personality theory. In effect, the very people who might be best able to provide systematic investigations concerning the worth of personality assessment often have turned to different areas of research.

The new clinical psychology tends to focus on treatments, and it has been a confusing and wondrous experience to note the remarkable accumulation of fads concerning treatment that have been generated during the past two decades, most likely with the objective of enticing new clientele or explaining treatment failures. New propositions about entities such as borderlines, anorexia, bulimia, obsessive compulsive disorders, panic disorders, multiple personalities, anxiety reactions, anti-social personalities, post traumatic stress disorders, and the like, have created a cadre of specialists in those disorders. These specialists often suggest that their credentials provide an implicit promise of cure, or at least a clear understanding of the problem.

Unfortunately, personality assessment has played an almost negligible role in contributing to these propositions, and research concerning these issues struggles to reach even a mediocre level. Stated simply, people who purport themselves to specialize in the treatment of these disorders have little interest in personality assessment for, by their logic, they already know what is wrong with the prospective patient and have the methodology readily available for correction. This unreasonable logic neglects the individual as a unique entity, and even more important, is based on the naive assumption that symptom presentation dictates a specific form of treatment. In effect, it is an extension of the medical-model to which many professional psychologists seem to object so strenuously.

This situation has been clouded further by the fact that many psychologists who practice intervention seem to be motivated by the general premise that it is more important to entice the subject to become a paying client, or a client for whom someone else will pay, rather than to be concerned with what is really wrong with the subject and/or what is really best for the subject. Sadly, a substantial number of psychologists practicing in the clinical area perceive themselves to be therapists and have settled upon one or, at most, two methods of intervention with which they feel comfortable employing with each potential patient, and they apparently are not very interested in personality assessment.

However, it is also important to note that even those who do personality testing often do not maximize the use of their findings. In a recent study in the United States (Exner, 1994), the names of 600 psychologists were selected randomly from the Directory of the National Register of Health Service Providers. This was done with the purpose of attempting to learn more about the interest in, or practice of personality assessment by those working in the field, especially those who treat patients in private practice. To that end, the random selection was restricted to those whose addresses appeared to be residential or office, that is, none were selected who's addresses included a university, hospital, or obvious state, city, or county mental health installation.

A brief twelve item questionnaire was sent together with a stamped, return envelope. Each question was stated in a manner that could be answered by selecting one of four options (1) never, (2) sometimes, (3) often (4) always. The first of the 12 questions asked whether the respondent administered (or had administered by someone else) personality testing prior to the third treatment session. The second question asked whether personality test results were used to plan treatment, such as deciding on treatment objectives, selecting a method of treatment, deciding on long term versus short term intervention, etc. The third question asked if the test results were used to formulate a diagnosis, and the remaining questions focused on the use of specific tests. Two of those questions concerned the use of the Rorschach and two concerned the use of the MMPI.

A total of 388 (65%) of the questionnaires were returned. Although the return is less than desirable, the data are quite striking and seem to send a message to those vested in personality assessment, and especially for those who are concerned with quality treatment planning.

Eighty-nine of the 388 respondents (23%) indicate that they never use personality testing. Sixty-two of the 89 indicate that they do not find them useful, and/or believe that they are invalid. Twenty of the 89 indicate that they are not sufficiently trained in their use. Seven of the 89 indicate that clients object to their use.

The remaining 299 respondents indicate that they do use personality testing, but only 201 of the 299 (67%) indicate that they use the results in planning treatment. This represents only 52% of the total number who responded.

One hundred eighty-four (92%) of the 201 respondents who do use test results for treatment planning always use a sentence completion blank and the remaining 17 respondents indicate that they use a SCB often.

One hundred twenty-three (61%) of the 201 respondents who use test results for treatment planning use the MMPI at times (sometimes = 34; often = 42; always = 28). Stated differently, about 32% of the total number of respondents use the MMPI, at times, to plan intervention.

One hundred twelve (51%) of the respondents who use test results to plan treatment administer the Rorschach at times (sometimes = 26; often

14

= 56; always = 30). This represents on 29% of the total number of respondents.

Interestingly, 99 of the 112 who use the Rorschach often or always for treatment planning also use the MMPI often or always. Similarly, and 92 of the 123 who use the MMPI often or always for treatment planning also use the Rorschach often or always. These seem to be the people who are invested in the use of personality assessment for purposes of treatment planning, but collectively, they constitute a relatively modest proportion of the total group, only about 49% of those who use test results for treatment planning, about 39% of all respondents who do use personality tests, and only 26% of the total number of respondents.

There is no way to know about the testing practices of the 212 non-responders but an ominous guess seems reasonable. In some respects, this lackadasical approach to treatment planning is an unethical disservice to people. Psychologists can and should do much better but, thus far, that does not seem to be the case. The fault is not with the lack of reliable and/or valid tests, although this is not to suggest that psychology has reached the ultimate in precision concerning the best ways to assess personality or to detect the often subtly unique features that mark people and differentiate each from the other. Nonetheless, currently available personality tests are reasonably sophisticated. Findings from them, especially those such as the Rorschach which yield very individualized findings, can be used logically and empirically to generate realistic intervention plans if the data are used wisely, and in the context of a cost-benefit-analysis that will require the least investment by the subject.

Some have argued that personality testing is time consuming and that the same information will ultimately be revealed as treatment progresses. Actually, the procedures involved usually take no more than a few hours if done by those competently trained in assessment. What person who submit himself or herself to surgery or some other form of drastic medical intervention without first being assurred that all available tests had been completed and that the attending physician was thoroughly aware of the issues involved and had considered all treatment alternatives? Do people seeking mental health attention deserve any less?

A simple illustration may be useful. It is taken from two real life cases. In this instance, the results are derived mainly from the Rorschach, and seem to affirm the importance of reviewing individual differences in treatment planning among patients who may have the same presenting symptomatology. The illustration involves two women, one age 27 and the second, age 32. Both presented themselves to potential therapists with vigorous complaints of frequent and disruptive bouts of anxiety and frequent panic attacks. They live in markedly disparate parts of the United States and each was assessed by a psychologist not known to the other.

The woman in Case 1 is separated after four years of marriage, while the Case 2 subject is single. Both have completed at least two years of college. The Case 1 subject currently works as a secretary in an accounting firm. The Case 2 subject currently works as a costume designer for a theatrical company. If either appeared before a consulting psychiatrist, there is a good likelihood that each would be prescribed some kind of anti-anxiety medication. If either appeared before a psychologist specializing in anxiety or panic reactions, it is likely that each would be subjected to some form of tension reduction treatment and stress management control. The question is whether the form of intervention might be different if the subjects were evaluated more thoroughly with regard to individual differences and unique personality characteristics. Both subjects were referred for personality assessment by their respective therapists, and bulk of the testing included the administration of a sentence completion blank and the Rorschach.

The psychologist responsible for the for the Case 1 assessment reports that the results indicate that subject is quite defensive, in spite of the fact that she has considerable resource, and that her capacities for control and tolerance for stress are usually as robust as those of most adults. However, these features currently are less effective because of some situationally related stress, which probably has to do with her recent separation. The effects of the stress are relatively modest, but they have created a state of psychological overload. This overload appears to have created a potential for impulsiveness that is more likely to manifest in her emotional displays than in her thinking. Much of her stress appears related to an experience of emotional loss and probably translates as feelings of loneliness or neglect. As a result, many of her psychological operations are more complex than usual and, although she appears to have a long standing confusion about her feelings, this confusion has become intensified.

It is also noted that she is an intensely self-centered individual who greatly overestimates her self-worth. A direct product of this tendency is to focus much more on herself than on others. As a result, her interpersonal relationships usually are more tenuous and less mature. Thus, emotional losses or rejections are likely to have a greater impact on her because she perceives them as insults to her over glorified sense of personal worth. Actually, her self concept is based much more on imagination than real experience. Nonetheless, it is important for her to defend her inflated sense of self and, because of this, she usually externalizes responsibility, especially for negative events and tends to avoid or deny unpleasantness.

She also has a strong passive-dependent orientation. She seems prone to seek relationships that are both supportive and nurturing. Unfortunately, this increases her vulnerability to the manipulations of others. It seems likely that she has some awareness of this and she seems considerably less secure about her interpersonal relations than are most people. She attempts to conceal or contend with these feelings of insecurity by using an intellectual, somewhat authoritarian approach to many issues. Although she is open to social interaction, she is cautious and sometimes even reluctant to initiate interpersonal exchanges, especially those that may require more tact and sophistication. She is especially defensive about relationships that may create unwanted demands on her or pose hazards to her control of the situation.

She an intuitive person, who is influenced greatly by her feelings when required to contend with demands for coping or decision making. Typically, she merges her feelings together with her thinking. She prefers to test out her decisions through trial and error activity and probably is not very reluctant to display her feelings. In fact, she may often convey the impression of being excessively emotional or even impulsive. Her thinking is usually clear but her current stress state tends to interfere with her abilities to concentrate or attend to specific events. Often, when in stress situations, she creates a self imposed form of helplessness in which she relies heavily on the actions of others for decision making. She has no major problems in reality testing and seems as prone as most adults to make conventional responses when the circumstances of the situation clearly define expected or acceptable answers. In effect, she is a somewhat hysteroid-like person who is currently foundering and having much difficulty her sometimes very intense feelings.

The report concerning the subject in Case 2 indicates that she is a very conservative and cautious person who seems quite insecure about herself and her ability to deal effectively with her world. She is especially reluctant to deal with complexity and has developed a basic orientation toward coping or decision making that causes her to be prone to keep things on a very simple and easily managed level. Although this coping style is not necessarily detrimental, it does serve to reinforce her notions that she is not very capable.

She is a very ideational person who prefers to stop and think things through before reaching a decision or initiating behaviors, but unfortunately, she commits much of her thinking to the development of fantasy, which she uses frequently and often abusively to avoid the stresses of reality. Although her capacities for control are quite adequate she is vulnerable to disorganization under stress because she really has fewer resources readily available than do most adults. She is quite conservative about processing new information and seems especially fearful of her feelings in decision making situations. As a result, she tries to avoid emotionally provocative situations whenever possible. In fact, she often goes to the extreme of emotionally isolating herself from close relations with others to avoid the quandries of dealing directly with her feelings.

Overall, she is a somewhat psychologically impoverished, relatively fragile, and somewhat schizoidish individual who does not regard herself very favorably. She seems forced to defend herself in an overly complicated world by assuming a passive or submissive interpersonal role. Although she is interested in people, her conceptions of them are based much more on her experiences from her fantasy life than from real experience. Thus, although she is open to closeness, she seems bewildered about how best this might be achieved and concerned about what sacrifices she might be called upon to make in return. The result is a person who tends to live on the periphery of her environment, seemingly aware of what goes on, but unable to partake in deep or mature relationships.

The psychologist reporting on the findings for Case 1 issues a convincing argument that the findings clearly point to a need for some form of supportive intervention to assist in working through the current stress situation created by the separation. The findings also highlighted to stress the importance of her strong passive-dependant orientation in planning for a supportive routine. The report also emphasizes the tendency of the subject to externalize cause, and the sometimes apparent volatility manifest in the overt expression of her feelings as potential targets for intervention, but cautions that these issues probably will not be open to treatment unless a longer term form of intervention, ideally, a developmental model of treatment, can evolve from the supportive intervention. The report notes that she has several assets that can be used to facilitate treatment. She has considerable resource. She has a relatively consistent coping style. She makes a serious effort to process information and ordinarily, she does not distort perceptual inputs. Her thinking is reasonably clear and she obviously has no negative sets toward her environment.

The psychologist writing the assessment report concerning the Case 2 subject argues convincingly that most of all her symptoms have evolved because she seems to live a very fragile existence, depending upon others with whom she is not really close and not being able to predict how effective or ineffective her avoidance style may be in her everyday living. When she is viewed as a unique person, optimal intervention objectives seem easily identified but an actual intervention strategy is more difficult to define than for Case 1. First, she must be approached very cautiously. It seems clear that this woman suffers enormously from many developmental problems. She is not sure who or what she is, and seems equally confused about others. Her resources are more limited than would be expected and her abusive use of fantasy serves only to sustain her impoverished plight. She is the type of person who, if confronted with the need for some long term form of treatment, is likely to bolt because the prospect could be too threatening. Thus, it may be more appropriate to broach the treatment issue in a more specific but open-ended way, possibly by suggesting a focus on broadening social skills and contending with feelings more directly to ease some of her symptoms. It seems also logical to caution the therapist about her avoidant and oversimplifying orientation and her abusive of fantasy. Both will clearly cause problems in treatment but the former will tend to interfere most, especially when complex issues are addressed.

If the same therapist were to treat both of these clients, using similar treatment tactics with both, it is possible that success might achieved with one and not the other, but it is also possible that, if the treatment simply focused on anxiety reduction, neither would benefit. Stated differently, an intervention methodology that might work for one of these subjects could not be expected to work for the other. Even though their presenting symptoms are similar, they are very different psychological people and only an extreme optimist could believe that a singular form of treatment will profit both. One seems in need of some sort of supportive treatment that might evolve into longer term developmental treatment. The second clearly requires a more developmentally oriented form of intervention.

Although anecdotal, these illustrations afford some emphasis to the importance of personality assessment, to understand the individual more thoroughly, and to plan treatment more realistically. It is true that many issues concerning the assessment of personality and the efficacy of the Rorschach remain open to inquiry. Research about personality and personality assessment has slowed, mainly because those in the professional areas of psychology have shunned those who may be in the best position to study the predictive value of personality assessment, that is, those vested mainly in research. Thus, unfortunately, assessment as a specialty, and Rorschach use in particular, is almost data-less in terms of predicting response to specific intervention models. Some data, scattered here and there, do exist, (Applebaum, 1977; Exner & Sanglade, 1992; Gerstle, Geary, Himmelstein & Reller-Geary, 1988; LaBarbera & Cornsweet (1985); Weiner & Exner, 1991), but the accumulated findings fall far short of offering a convincing need for assessment, or the use of the Rorschach in most or all cases.

It is also obvious that personality assessment can also be used to evaluate treatment outcome, but that is a far less common practice than should be the case, and data concerning this process is almost nonexistent.

If personality assessment, and Rorschach use in particular, is to be respected and successful into the next century, the purpose should be defined more concisely than seems to have been the case. Training in assessment, and especially in the Rorschach may be at fault. The Rorschach, or for that matter, any personality assessment instrument, should not be administered as part of an esoteric exercise. Often, students are trained how to administer and interpret the test, but sometimes, they are not taught how to use the resulting data to the fullest extent. Students training in the Rorschach should be taught to use the test wisely and in the context of the purpose for which the assessment is designed. If an emphasis on logically developed treatment planning is provided, the procedures will make more sense, not only to students, but to colleagues in psychology and psychiatry, and this will reaffirmed the expertise and integrity of the special skills available from the well trained clinician.

Résumé

L'histoire du Rorschach indique que l'intérêt pour le test s'est accru régulièrement, mais qu'il s'est essentiellement centré sur deux questions fondamentales: (a) comment fonctionne le test, et (b) comment on peut utiliser le test pour différencier des groupes d'individus entre eux, les schizophrènes des dépressifs par exemple. Ces domaines d'investigation sont certes très importants, mais on a moins directement abordé la question de l'individualité, c'estàdire ce qui fait que les personnes diffèrent, tout en se ressemblant par certains côtés. En laissant de côté cet aspect important, on risque fort de limiter la qualité des recommandations de traitement qu'on pourrait être amené à faire à partir des résultats du test, et même de les empêcher tout à fait.

La pratique du psychodiagnostic, qui consiste à évaluer le fonctionnement d'une personnalité à l'aide d'une batterie de test, a toujours été plus qu'une recherche d'étiquette diagnostique. De manière implicite, on considérait que les informations obtenues sur le sujet pourraient contribuer à son bienêtre thérapeutique. On constate malheureusement aujourd'hui qu'un nombre considérable de psychologues cliniciens se perçoivent comme des thérapeutes et choisissent de pratiquer une ou deux méthodes d'intervention qui leur conviennent, sans se demander si ces tactiques d'intervention sont les plus appropriées au sujet. Et même ceux qui pratiquent effectivement les tests psychologiques dans une visée individualisante ne savent pas toujours mettre à profit les résultats. Une enquête récente portant sur les pratiques d'évaluation a montré que 23% des psychologues qui effectuent des thérapies n'utilisent jamais des tests de personnalité. Sur les 77% restant, qui pratiquent l'examen psychologique, deuxtiers seulement déclarent utiliser les résultats pour les indications de traitement, et pas plus de deuxtiers disent utiliser le Rorschach.

Il est évident qu'une indication thérapeutique ne peut pas reposer uniquement sur la symptomatologie présentée, sauf dans des cas très particuliers. Chaque personne diffère de manière significative de toutes les autres personnes et elle est en droit de supposer que l'on a procédé à une évaluation rigoureuse avant de la diriger vers telle ou telle forme de traitement. Qui serait assez fou pour se soumettre à une opération chirurgicale ou à quelque autre forme d'intervention médicale radicale sans s'assurer d'abord que tous les tests nécessaires ont été effectués, que le médecin concerné est parfaitement conscient des tenants et des aboutissants, et qu'il a considéré toutes les alternatives thérapeutiques?

La recherche sur la personnalité marque le pas, et on trouve très peu de recherches sur le Rorschach et l'évaluation qui permettraient d'anticiper la réactivité des sujets à des modes spécifiques d'intervention. Si l'on veut que l'évaluation de la personnalité et l'utilisation du Rorschach soient à la fois respectées et pertinentes dans le siècle à venir, il est nécessaire d'en clarifier plus avant les objectifs. Si l'on voulait bien s'attacher à développer de manière logique des stratégies de traitement, alors les procédures seraient plus compréhensibles et le Rorschach pourrait trouver son plein emploi en contribuant à la santé de nos clients.

Resumen

La historia del Rorschach indica que el interés en la prueba ha venido aumentando de manera continua, pere tendiendo a centrarse en dos temas principales: (a) cómo trabaja el test y (b) cómo puede ser utilizado para diferenciar grupos de personas, tales come esquizofrénicos de depresivos.

Aunque estas áreas de interés son importantes, al tema de la individualidad—es decir, cómo las personas difieren aunque se asemejen en algunos aspectos—se le ha prestado menor atención. El descuido de este importante aspecto de la pruebe limita con frecuencia la calidad de las recomendaciones deducidas de los hallazgos respecto a la planificación del tratamiento, llegando incluso a impedir que se derive contribution alguna en ese sentido.

El procedimiento llamado psicodiagnóstico—evaluar el funcionamiento de la personalidad con una batería de pruebas clinicas—no se limitaba a la búsqueda de una etiqueta diagnóstica. Se suponía, de manera implícita, que la información acerca del sujeto contribuiría a su bienestar por intermedio de la psicoterapia. Lamentablemente, una cantidad sustancial de psicólogos que practican hoy en al área clínica y se perciben a si mismos como terapeutas se han instalado en uno o dos métodos de intervención con los cuales se sienten cómodos, independientemente de si tales tácticas de intervención son las más apropiadas. Aún aquellos que sí utilizan pruebas de personalidad focalizando en el individua, con frecuencia no explotan cabalmente sus hallazgos. En una encuesta reciente acerca de la práctica de evaluación de las personalidad, 23% de los psicólogos que hacen tratemiento indicaron no usar nunca pruebas de personalidad. Del 77% restante que sí lo hacen, solo dos tercios indicaron que utilizaban los resultadols para la planificación del tratamiento, y sólo alrededor de dos tercios reportaron user el Rorschach.

Resulta obvio que la planificación del tratamiento no puede basarse únicamente en la presencia de síntomas, excepto en circunstancias insulares. Los personas difieren significativamente y tienen el derecho a ser evaluadas de manera integral, antes de iniciar cualquier forma particular de tratamiento. Quién se sometería a una cirugía, u otra forma radical de intervención médica, sin que se le asegurase previamente que today las pruebas disponibles habrían sido relizadas, y que el médico tratante estaría plenamente consciente de las cuestiones en juego y considerado todas las alternativas de tratamiento?

   Las investigaciones sobre la personalidad han disminuido, y escasean particularmente las investigaciones en evaluación con el Rorschach que permitan realizar predicciones sobre la respuesta a modos especificos de intervención. El respecto y éxito que logren la evaluación de la personalidad y el Rorschach en el siglo próximo dependen de que el propósito que complen se establezca con mayor claridad. Se se have énfasis en al desarollo lógico de la planificación del tratamiento, los procedimientos tendrán mayor sentido y las contribuciones del Rorschach al bienestar de nuestros clientes podrán ser aprovechadas a plenitud.

References

Allport, G. W. (1937). *Personality: A psychological interpretation*. New York: Holt, Rinehart & Winston.

Applebaum, S. (1977). *Anatomy of change*. New York: Plenum.

Exner, J. E. (in press). Why use personality tests: A brief history and some comments. In J. N. Butcher (Ed.), *Practical considerations in clinical personality assessment*. New York: Oxford University Press.

Exner, J. E., & Andronikof-Sanglade, A. (1992). Rorschach changes following brief and short-term therapy. *Journal of Personality Assessment, 59*, 59–71.

Gerstle, R. M., Geary, D. C., Himmelstein, P., & Reller-Geary, L. (1988). Rorschach predictors of therapeutic outcome for inpatient treatment of children: A proacticve study. *Journal of Clinical Psychology, 44*, 277–280.

LaBarbera, J. D., & Cornsweet, C. (1985). Rorschach predictors of therapeutic outcome in a child psychiatric inpatient service. *Journal of Personality Assessment, 49*, 120–124.

Murray, H. A. (1938). *Explorations in pesonality*. New York: Oxford University Press.

Weiner, I. B., & Exner, J. E. (1991). Rorschach changes in long-term and short term psychotherapy. *Journal of Personality Assessment, 56*, 453–465.

The Rorschach and Other Projective Methods in Portugal

Danilo Silva

University of Lisbon, Portugal

Maria Emilia Marques

I.S.P.A., Portugal

It is not possible to speak about projective methods in Portugal, their study, application, research and teaching, without mentioning the general path that psychology has taken in our country. When its history is written, it will be possible to see the influence of several successive circumstances, among which stands out the nature of the political and ideological regime that governed this Portugal for most of this century.

Up until the 1930s there were several individuals, mostly university professors, who paid close attention to trends in psychology in other countries, most visibly in the field of education. Nevertheless, there were also important scholars whose names are attached to various centers and institutions around the country who were interested in the areas of the school and professional counselling, general child psychology, mental retardation, and clinical and forensic psychology.

Experimental Psychology was the first area in which university teaching was allowed, beginning early in this century with an experimental psychology class. In 1911, Lisbon's and Coimbra's Colleges of Arts were created, and the experimental psychology class and its laboratory were assigned to the philosophy curriculum. This situation persisted until 1957, when a new course on general psychology was introduced under the name of "Introduction to Psychology." Under this 1957 curriculum reform, students could take the experimental and the introduction to psychology courses in their first and fourth years, and they could also enroll in a final psychology seminar and prepare their dissertation on psychology. This kind of organization allowed the regular publication of essays, research, and papers in Lisbon where, from 1951 to 1970, 78 titles can be counted. One must note the interest of the medical colleges in psychology subjects; in 1955, the Medical Psychology subject was introduced in their curricula.

The need for a degree in psychology was deeply felt by now; the 1940s witnessed movements and proposals voiced by Moreira de Sá, a professor in the Lisbon College of Arts, who had recently arrived from studying in the United States. But all of these efforts were in vain. One of the last occurred in 1968, when the Ministry of Education created a psychology degree in the Lisbon University. However, the minister was replaced and his successor did not ratify the law. That decision was most certainly influenced by the May, 1968 student movements in Paris, where psychology students stood up to be recognized in the events that shook De Gaulle.

The 1960s in Portugal witnessed the colonial war that, apparently, was intended to stop pressures for independence. Almost every young man was drafted and left home for one of the colonies. It was a war ordered by a decaying regime of very old men, condemned by the young, namely, the university students who understood neither the objectives nor the values involved and whose ideas diverged from those of people who supported the war. During these years the student protest movements were constant and faced several restrictions of free speech, reading, writing, and gathering. They were also asked to sacrifice 3 or more years of life in the compulsory military draft if not to give up life itself.

It was in the beginning of this troubled decade, in 1962, that an association of religious catholic congregations founded the first school of psychology in Portugal, the Instituto Superior de Psicologia Aplicada (ISPA), in Lisbon, whose aim was to provide training for the numerous teachers of private religious schools for which they were responsible for all over the country. We can very well think that the religious nature of the promoters of this initiative had a crucial influence on its approval. In fact, the Catholic Church never openly defied the regime; the regime, in turn, hoped for, and found, an ally, in the Church. In 1964, the Institute admitted laymen and underwent several curricula changes until, in 1973, its curricula was recognized as a degree program by the education ministry.

Interest in assessment grew during this period of time. The Portuguese Psychological Society formed in 1965 and, 2 years later, launched the first issue of its review *Revista Portuguesa de Psicologia*; in 1966, a study group separated from the Luso-Spanish Psychoanalytic

Society and later originated the Portuguese Psychoanalytic Society that, in 1981, was integrated into the International Psychoanalytic Society; the first Medical-Pedagogic Observation Center was created, and psychology entered the Forces in the first Army Psychotecnical Studies Center; industrial psychology started, as did the first orientation and selection centers. These and other phenomena reflected an urgency for scientific training that could answer to the deeply felt lack in the various sectors of life and social organization.

In 1977 Psychology degrees (Licenciaturas em Psicologia) were created in Lisbon, Coimbra, and Porto, and they were given the status of Colleges of Psychology Colleges in 1981. More recently a degree in psychology was established at Minho University in the city of Braga. Also in recent years, several private institutions have established training departments in such other areas as health, educational, and organizational psychology.

The Instituto Superior de Psicologia Aplicada (ISPA) was developed and in time provided expanded training for psychologists. In 1974 its ownership by the Catholic Religious Institute that created it ceased. It then revised its curricula and hired new and better qualified teachers trained in different areas of specialization in Portugal and abroad. Presently its diplomas constitute a degree that has been recognized officially since 1986.

The Projective Methods

Where do projective methods stand in all of this? We lack sufficient research to show how, where, and by whom these instruments were brought to Portugal and who did the first theoretical work, research, and practice on them. Where the Rorschach is concerned, we do know that the first publication dates back to 1938. It is an article by Luís de Pina, Professor at the Porto medical college and director of the Criminal Institute in the same city, and it is titled "O Psicodiagnóstico de Rorschach em Criminologia" (Rorschach Psychodiagnosis in Criminology) (1938). We read the following in this article: "The Rorschach *test*, up to now, has not been used in Portugal as the subject of any research. As far as I know, it has not penetrated the most appropriate circles: Psychiatry and Criminology" (Pina, 1938). This quotation suggests to us that Rorschach had been known and used in this country, but that this was the first time

26

it was applied in research. As for an indication of the most appropriate settings in which it should be used, we could comment accurately only if we had fuller information about the development of psychology and related sciences at the time. The Pina study is significant for presenting Rorschach research for the first time in Portugal. Incidentally, we might mention that the suggestion of criminology as a fruitful field for Rorschach applications has been underscored by the bibliography of the last two decades.

Psychiatrist Almada Araújo, Director of the National Vocational Counselling Institute, was probably the first Portuguese member of the International Rorschach Society. He introduced and extensively used the Rorschach in clinical work and counselling during the 1940s and 1950s. Ana Gonzalez belonged to the same Institute. We do not know of any publications by these practitioners.

Graphic projective tests were also known at this time. They were used and studied in the Instituto António Aurélio da Costa Ferreira, and we can find references to them in some papers included in their internationally well known magazine in the 1950s and the 1960s, "A Criança Portuguesa."

Projective methods were known and studied in limited areas of the Universities. Among psychology dissertations from 1951–1970, we can find 11 on projective methods: TAT, Tree test, Fay's drawing test, Goodenough test, Rorschach, Tile test, and McClelland's Thematic Apperceptive method. The fact that these graphic tests stand out is explained by the fact that child psychology had become comparatively well-developed in the middle of a generally poor national situation. However, the early workers did not have the power to create a Rorschach movement or to develop an area of study, practice, and research on projective methods.

Teaching

It was not until the middle of the 1960s and perhaps even later that specific teaching of projective theory and methods had its start. In 1967, a regular annual class was begun in ISPA. Rorschach, Szondi, and TAT were the main subjects in the first years, mainly for the clinical area students. During the 1970s, due to changes in curricula and teachers, this class did not continue except for the Rorschach.

The last ISPA curricula reorganization, in 1981, provided for specific attention to projective methods and stable ways of teaching them. The

ISPA curricula currently includes a third year semester course on introduction to projective methods. It focuses on the theoretical bases of projective methodology and introduces the Rorschach test, its characteristics, areas of use, application rules, and codification. The ISPA curricula also includes for the clinical students a fourth year semester course on Rorschach and another semester on TAT. In the fifth year, and also for the clinical students, there is an annual optional subject intended to offer deeper study of projective psychology. In this seminar, for 2 hours a week, protocols taken by the students and the theory of projective techniques are subject to careful study. Compulsory research for the final thesis has yielded a great number of studies using projective methods.

Official recognition, in 1991, of ISPA's Master degree in psychopathology and clinical psychology put the Rorschach again in the core of the study of methods of psychological assessment.

In Colleges of Psychology, teaching of projective methodology has been conditioned by availability of the necessary specifically trained teachers. In Lisbon, the reference to projective methods and their study has been constant, although limited, within the psychology degree. Annual courses on the Rorschach were held in the years following the fall of the dictatorship in 1974, a political circumstance that allowed very active organization of the psychology university degree. But curricula organization for the three university psychology degrees led to the integration of projective methods study in the subjects of differential psychology and personality assessment techniques at the University of Lisbon, university, where it is only one of the topics taught.

During more than 10 years of his practice, teaching, and research with the Rorschach and the TAT, Danilo Silva's assistant was Isabel Fernandes, who arrived from the University of Paris in 1979, where they both did post-graduate work in psychopathology and projective techniques. In 1985, in Lisbon, two optional courses devoted to the Rorschach were established by Silva, who introduced the Rorschach Comprehensive System in Portugal and has taught it since then in the College of Psychology at the University of Lisbon. A psychologist educated at the University of Lyon, Abel Pires, who now teaches at the University of Porto, became interested in this new development and also took up the Comprehensive System in place of the French method. After being introduced to the system and attending a workshop in Madrid given by Exner himself, Pires went to the University of South Florida to participate in workshops and acquire a deeper knowledge of Rorschach practice, analysis, and interpretation, under the supervision of I. B. Weiner.

Returning to Porto, he introduced the teaching of the Comprehensive System in the third year of the psychology degree course in intelligence and personality assessment. Even before going to Florida, however, he had the opportunity to teach introductory courses on the Comprehensive System to undergraduate and graduate psychology students and prepare them to use the test in research he was conducting. One of these students was Miguel Gonçalves, now an Assistant Professor in the Minho University program, where he introduced the Comprehensive System as well.

Professor Castro Fonseca from Coimbra University informs us that projective techniques are studied as a fourth year subject in which teaching of the Rorschach occupies one semester. This is a compulsory subject in the clinical psychology area and an optional subject for other students. A third year course on methods of psychological observation and assessment is taught to all students and includes some coverage of the Rorschach. Aura Montenegro, who coordinates these courses, has translated and adapted the Burstein and Loucks "Manual for the Interpretative Codification of the Rorschach Test" used by her graduate students.

The small place that projective methodology occupies in the psychology degree program and the lack of post-graduate education to this day has led many of the faculty in these programs to offer courses on an extra-curricular basis. Courses on the Rorschach, TAT, Zulliger, and Szondi are often requested by private practitioners in psychology and by welfare, vocational, and personnel selection agencies.

We would like to call attention to some training courses sponsored by the Portuguese Society of Rorschach and Projective Methods, a Society created in 1982. These courses were held in Lisbon and Coimbra and were organized by Víctor Moita and António Diniz. Some were devoted to the Rorschach and were taught by Lúcia Coelho, Frieda Rossel, and Víctor Moita; others concerned the Zulliger and were conducted by Víctor Moita; still others addressed the TAT and were given by Maria Emília Marques.

A Section on Personality Assessment created within the Portuguese Psychological Society in 1990 has also organized seminars intended to enhance understanding Rorschach interpretation following the Comprehensive System. The first of these was conducted in 1988 by Concepción Sendín, the Rorschach Workshops Spanish representative. The next year the seminar focused on the Rorschach and defense mechanisms and involved techniques for analyzing these mechanisms and included analysis of two protocols of individuals with borderline personality structures. The seminars in 1990, 1991, and 1992 were devoted fully to the protocol interpretation. Last year and in January 1993, two workshops were held, one by Exner and the other by Weiner, which were dedicated to recent research data and advances in interpretation and allowed us to update our concepts. Weiner's workshop emphasized the use of the Rorschach in forensic cases.

In Lisbon, Silva and Prazeres accepted an invitation from the Portuguese Society of Clinical Psychology to organize courses for psychologists on the Comprehensive System, which started in 1992. Bruno Gonçalves, Professor the University of Lisbon, began an interesting program of teaching the Szondi test in the Instituto Jacob Rodrigues Pereira to psychologists who work with profoundly deaf children and youths.

These observations show that the projective methodology has attracted fairly substantial interest and is in demand by psychologists, especially those who are psychodynamically trained. At the same time, the Portuguese Rorschach Society and the Section on Personality Assessment have concerned themselves with the improvement and consolidation of the teaching and knowledge of the main projective methods, as is evidenced by the visit to Portugal of leading specialists from different theoretical backgrounds.

Research

The research developed on projective methods in Portugal in these last decades is not yet fully appreciated. However, it is fair to say that this research consists mainly of isolated papers that provide little continuity.

The growing number of young psychologists travelling to foreign universities since the 1960s has stimulated this research and begun to promote some continuity in the studies. Silva's bibliographic research on the TAT, under the supervision of Shentoub, is an extensive reading guide on this method; it stemmed from a gathering of texts and data closely related to the psychoanalytic views of that French author. As the TAT method was not well known in Portugal, the author tried to direct his work in a way that could introduce readers to the American bibliography and give them a worthwhile exposure to the method.

The first part of that publication, entitled "A Psychoanalytic Perspective on the Interpretation of the TAT" (Silva, 1971), presents Murray's main personology ideas, namely, the projection and apperception concepts that led to the development of the TAT. In the second part of his work, Silva presents some basic concepts of ego psychology that seemed to him better suited to TAT interpretation, drawn from the work of such scholars as Hartmann, Rapaport, Kris, Schafer, Holt, and Bellak. He then goes on to present suggestions for interpretation, the last of which follows Shentoub. The study concludes with a review of publications concerning the TAT process and including viewpoints on the nature of the TAT responses, extending from fantasies such as dreams to the cognitive responses themselves and including Wyatt's "induced fantasy" notion shared by Shentoub.

In this regard one can also find in the Portuguese bibliography such papers on projective methods as "Analysis of Studies on Rorschach Validity in Clinical Psychology" (Silva, 1982); "Projective Techniques: Some Thoughts" (Silva, 1986); and "The Rorschach Test: Some Points Related To Criticisms and New Perspectives on Utilization" (Pires, 1986).

Ph. D. Theses

Among studies of projective methodology, either published or not, university Ph. D. theses bear witness to the interest in this area of study and bring quality and significance to the work being done. In chronological order of presentation to the University of Lisbon, first is Silva's study *The Apperception Test for Children (Human Figures)–CAT-H: A Normative Study*. This is a use of the CAT-H with 100 children of both sexes, 6–10 years old, without psychological disturbance and displaying a 90–115 WISC-IQ. The first two chapters focus on apperception-thematic techniques for children, such as Blum's Blacky Pictures, Shneidman's Make-A-Picture-Story (MAPS), and Corman's Pata Negra, and provide a more detailed account of Bellak's CAT-A and CAT-H.

After brief comments on the meaning of and need for normative studies on projective techniques, the author goes on to explain his research methodology. The next two rather long chapters analyze stories from the thematic and apperceptive points of view. Based on Rosenzweig and Fleming's method of analysis, the author proceeds to the record the apperceptive data on each card for the male and female sub-groups and then for a normative group at each level by sex for the whole sample. A chapter on thematic norms uses the same approach, as suggested by

31

Eron's list of themes. A final chapter presents the analysis, distribution and normative data for each card, the length of the stories and the time used to tell them, silences within story telling, the need to question the examiner on clarification or story extent, and the latency of the initial response. Then the author presents the results for the male and female sub-groups expressed in means, medians, and standard deviations, with a discussion of differences among sexes. This study was published in 1982 by the Instituto Nacional de Investigação Científica (Silva, 1982).

In 1982 Moita presented in the René Décartes University (Sorbonne) a Ph.D. study entitled *Modalités de Réponses au Rorschach et Statut Sociométriques chez les Pré-Adolescents: Contribuition à l'Étude de la Personnalité du Garçon Pubère*. This study examines 72 pre-adolescent boys, 13–15 years old, classified according to Moreno's sociometric status technique. The author wished to identify Rorschach variables associated with characteristic patterns of overt behavior in the different sociometric status groups contained in the sample. The presentation begins by stating the problem and discussing inter-individual models of inter-personal relationships and sociometric status. A brief chapter on pre-adolescent development follows. Then the Rorschach is presented with respect to the nature of the response process as conceived in the French psychoanalytic theory of Rausch de Traubenberg, Widlöcher, and others. The fifth chapter presents and discusses the normative data that were obtained. The author concludes with a discussion of the Rorschach results in relation to the subjects' sociometric status.

Francisco C. Carneiro presented his Ph.D. at the University of Paris VII in 1986; the title was *Le Test de l'Arbre: une Approche Dynamique*. The study begins with an introduction to drawing as a projective technique; the author speaks about the origins of and the research done with the Tree Test and provides a critical evaluation of its applications and normative data.

The second part of the thesis presents the theoretical basis of the test and continues with the administration of the instrument and the characteristics of the sample studied. The sample was obtained the Paris outskirts and comprised two groups: an experimental group of 72 psychotic adolescent boys, 12–17 years old, and a control group of 72 normal subjects. Next there is a chapter on the analysis of the drawings and coding criteria; results follow, with each codification item commented on the performance of each group. The results indicate an evolution in the development of drawing over time in the normal group but not in the psychotic group.

The third part of the thesis is a case study, an in the fourth part the author presents data related to a new tree drawing theory. The author discusses administration instructions that should, according to him, give subjects complete freedom to draw the tree of their choice without restrictions. Carneiro also comments on tree drawing as an optimal relation situation and on the theme of the projection linked to the so called "dreamed tree." Besides being a valuable piece of research, this work has been of particular interest to Portuguese psychologists who use graphic projective tests, especially the tree drawing, because of the theoretical framework that it presents (Carneiro, 1985).

In 1989 B. Gonçalves presented at the Catholic University of Louvain, in Belgium, a Ph. D. thesis entitled *La Squizophrenie à travers le Test de Szondi*. In this study the author presents and defines the Szondi test and the theory of pulsions that underlies it, and he discusses its relationship to schizophrenia. He also clarifies his own views on the Freudian and Jungian concepts of projection and inflation. The sample he used for his research comprised two groups: an experimental group of Portuguese recent onset schizophrenic subjects, mean age of 26 years, and a "normal" group comparable in sex, age, educational level, and nationality. The author hoped to demonstrate (a) that one could globally discriminate the Szondi responses of the two groups, and (b) that *Sch* Vector of the "Ego" plays an important role in that distinction. He also wanted to clarify which of the p (egosyntonic) factor tendencies, inflation (p+) or projection (p-), is more closely related to schizophrenia. The cluster analysis method that he used showed that not only one can clearly distinguish the two groups but can also define them differently. The *Sch* Vector stand out mainly by virtue of its p factor. The data also suggested that the schizophrenic sample had three subgroups and the "normal" sample four subgroups. Finally, it was possible to verify a structural relationship between schizophrenic disturbance and the "inflative" position of the self.

In 1992 Teresa Fagulha presented at the University of Lisbon a Ph. D. thesis with the title *A Prova "Era uma vez . . . " Uma Prova Projectica para Criances* (1992). This was a new projective test for children involving story completion. The stories are presented in three cartoon episodes, and the child must choose from among nine small scenes and put them in sequence to tell a story; the child must then tell the story that he or she has created with the scenes. The test is composed of seven cards, each showing a cartoon story, and one card for training. There are masculine and feminine versions that are alike except for a child-character that is a boy in the first and a girl in the second version.

This test aims to describe how children elaborate emotions, mainly anxiety and pleasure, that are fundamental affects in psychological adaptation. Five of the stimulus cards present anxiety situations that occur frequently in childhood experience, and two of them present rather pleasant events. The decision to include pleasant situation stimuli seemed appropriate due to the diagnostic importance of information concerning how children react to positive events.

The author drew on psychodynamic formulations of the function of play to present the hypothesis that the test material (cartoon stories) and the task of constructing the stories could be a creative experience, similar to the one that occurs in Winnicott's transitional space. In that creative space, children elaborate emotional experiences that can re-create and control the balance between fantasy and reality. Thus, for each stimulus cartoon, the author created nine small scene cards that can constitute a continuation of the story. These nine cards can be grouped in three categories: anxiety (three small cards depicting painful experiences); fantasy (three small cards depicting a pleasant event or a magical fantasy as relief and an alternative to the anxiety situation); and reality (three small cards depicting an effort to face an anxiety-provoking situation in children's real lives.

The characteristic of the cards chosen and the sequence in which they are placed to continue the story presented are the primary elements of interpretation, because they indicate how a child in the test situation tries to master anxiety evoked by the stimulus. The particular story the child relates also contributes important elements to the interpretation.

The test was studied with a group of 245 children, 6–8 years old. The frequency with which the different category scenes were chosen for each stimulus-card was studied according to the placement the child gave it (first, second, or third place in the sequence). The author also studied four groups of children with different behavioral characteristics (aggressive, hyperactive, anxious, isolated), and the results indicated that these four groups could be statistically differentiated from each other and from the control group.

Other Forms of Research

The ISPA has as a degree requirement the preparation of a monograph. This requirement has led to a large number of studies of uneven quality.

They are broad in scope, with respect to the samples they include, the themes they pursue, and the tests that they use. Among other topics, they have contributed something to the study of color; to studies of subjects in certain circumstances such as pregnancy, motherhood, infertility, and fetal death; and to studies with adolescents, the offspring of alcoholic or delinquent parents, anorexic adolescents, adults with depressive or schizophrenic symptoms, and psychosomatic patients. The Rorschach and TAT are the more common methods used, but there are also studies with CAT-A, the Pata Negra, and the Zulliger.

This is certainly a rich lode of studies, even though they do not always meet desired standards of research design; certainly they bear witness to the training and research that is likely to blossom in the near future. The ISPA's projective techniques research group is trying to preserve all of these works in order to classify them and save them from obscurity.

Currently this institution has formulated some specific research guidelines that we will summarize next. Studies of the Rorschach are designed with attention to the relationship between perception and projection; the aim is to study the characteristics of response formation as a symbol formation process. Attention is also paid to the concepts of "intersubjectivity" and "transformation" in the Rorschach situation and their close relation to the context in which the test is used. This line of investigation is addressed by Marques in her Ph.D. research and also by Pedro Aleixo, who is interested in the use of the "symmetry" concept in understanding the image construction process in the Rorschach.

There is one more thematic line of investigation to mention, led by Marques and concerned with male-female expression in adolescence in the Rorschach and TAT. This work is proceeding in two directions: trying to clarify the acquisition of gender-role identity through the relationship with mother and father, and trying to establish accurate indicators of though processes in adolescence. The work is trying to establish two fundamental lines, at the moment: one of them tries to clarify the sexualization path or the male-female identity acquisition through the relationship with mother and father; the other tries to establish accurate analysis indicators that might reveal thought process characteristics in adolescence.

Both of these lines of research derive from the French School of Rorschach and the theories of Freud, Melanie Klein, and post-Kleinian authors. Several papers have emerged from this research, some by Marques and others in which she is co-author (Marques, 1990–1992).

Víctor Moita is Professor at Porto University and has focused in recent years on study of the Zulliger. He is concerned in particular with the possibility of using the Zulliger in the psychological assessment of school age children and the study of child expressiveness (1983, 1988).

Other areas of study are now blossoming, including the work on motherhood and pregnancy and the research in psychosomatics and forensic psychology. An issue of the ISPA's Review "Análise Psicológica" currently in press is devoted entirely to forensic psychology. The projective techniques have an important place in this issue, especially the Rorschach.

In the Psychometric and Education Psychology Center at the University of Lisbon there is a research program exclusively dedicated to the study of projective methods and their use. The present members of this research time are Silva, Isabel Fernandes, Rosa Novo, and Nina Prazeres. Their collaboration has generated several publications.

Fernandes authored the first Portuguese article concerned with the Popular Responses (P) in the Rorschach, using the Hertz criteria that consider as Popular all responses occurring once in six protocols (Fernandes, 1977). In 1985 the Portuguese Society of Psychology held a commemoration of the 50th anniversary of the TAT; in that session, Fernandes read a paper entitled "The Thematic Apperception Test (TAT): Shentoub's Theory and Method, Presenting Six Protocols" (Fernandes, 1985). In a seminar on the Rorschach and defense mechanisms she also read a paper entitled "Narcissistic Functioning and Borderline Personality Organization in the Rorschach" (Fernandes, 1989). The research aims of this psychologist center on the analysis of similarities and differences in projection on the Rorschach and TAT. In a paper at the XIII Rorschach Congress in Paris, "Comparative Study of Projection in the Rorschach and the TAT of a Schizophrenic Group," Fernandes states that the analysis presented tends to reveal the complementarity of these two projective techniques. "Very often," she writes "only through the articulated reading of both techniques can the how and the *why* of a given functioning be clarified and justified. Even when the revealed psychological characteristic is the same in both techniques, their analysis shows how its manifestations are different in different performances" (Fernandes, 1991).

Novo conducted an interesting study with a group of female university students. She attempted to identify and analyze the expression of field dependence and independence in the Rorschach. She administered the Witkin Embedded Figures Test to 96 subjects and then gave the Rorschach to two groups: 31 subjects who were lowest third of the Witkin distribution field independents) and 29 subjects in the highest third (field dependents). Discriminant analysis using 13 Rorschach variables correctly placed 62% of 55 of the 60 subjects in their correct group (Novo, 1991).

After studying in Paris between 1969 and 1971 and earning the Projective Techniques Certificate with Rausch de Traubenberg and Shentoub, Silva undertook the study of 20 young adults, both male and female, with the Rorschach and the TAT, to ascertain whether both tests really identify personality structure (Silva, 1975). He then used Shentoub's story analysis sheet, which focuses on formal aspects of language and story telling. He examined only four Rorschach variables and four TAT variables. His discussion stresses the existence of an overlapping zone between the nature of the test and the underlying response process that can yield similar information.

Following his CAT-H study already mentioned, Silva published in 1983 a short study analyzing certain characteristic male-female responses to the CAT-H. He discusses differences between males and females on six structural characteristics related to apperceptive aspects and on five dynamic characteristics related to themes (Silva, 1983/1984).

In 1985, on the 50th anniversary of the TAT, Silva read a paper entitled "The TAT: Some Theoretical Issues and Perspectives on Its Use." The author reviews the old argument that the TAT, like most projective methods, does not belong to a particular personality theory, such as psychoanalytic theory. He indicates the possibility of using these instruments from a behavioral perspective and cites an article by Auld in this regard that appeared in the *Journal of Projective Techniques* (1954, *18*, 421–426). This issue is of the Journal was entirely dedicated to the subject of the multiplicity of theoretical perspectives on the use of projective techniques. Silva refers in particular to the cognitive perspective presented by Sobel in 1981 and to Bellak's categorization of ego functions in the early 1970s (Silva, 1985).

Since then, Silva's research has concentrated on introducing Exner's Rorschach Comprehensive System in Portugal. He published one paper that describes the origin and general features of the system and reviews the work of Exner and his collaborators on the response process and on reliability (Silva, 1986); a second paper, following the publication of the second edition of Volume 1 of the Comprehensive System addresses the nature of the test, its administration and norms, and several aspects of scoring leading to the steps in interpretation (Silva, 1986b).

At the XII International Congress of Rorschach in San Paulo, Silva presented a study that would guide his research for the next several years. This was an examination of temporal consistency in 30 school age children who were tested at the beginning of primary school and again 6 months later. The results generally agreed with those of Exner. Nevertheless, there were no high correlation values even though in 12 of 21 retest protocols the correlations reached significance at the .05 or .01 level, with m and Y among the lowest (Silva, 1987/88). However, the findings for some of the variables were surprising; in particular, the $X+\%$, $X-\%$, *Lambda*, and *W:D* showed results very different from those of Exner-Weiner. The Y determinants were more frequent than T, the $X+\%$ value was rather low, the $X-\%$ was rather high, the *Lambda* was often greater than 1.00, *Reflection Responses* (r) were absent, and the number of detail responses (D) exceeded the number of whole responses (W).

In a further examination of $X+\%$ and $X-\%$, the author tested two additional groups of boys and girls at the end of the first grade. These two groups were higher in socioeconomic level than those in the first study, and the third group was composed exclusively of high social class children. The third group was slightly higher in $X+\%$ than the other two groups, but not significantly so. Likewise, their $X-\%$ was lower than that of the other two groups, but not significantly. The other variables also showed similar findings for the most part (Silva, 1989, 1991). A third longitudinal study involved testing this second group annually for 3 years. The results demonstrated developmental changes over time on certain Rorschach variables while also emphasizing the importance of recognizing possible differences from the Exner-Weiner normative data in Portuguese children (Silva, 1992).

A study presented at the XIIIth International Rorschach Congress in Paris is related to this same issue of differences between Exner's results and normative data for the European population. This research involved 100 male and female subjects, mostly university educated. Although this was not a random sample, we nevertheless were struck by the same trend in some mean values, that is, lower form level and fewer T than Y. Although we do not want to attach too much importance to these results from a nonrandom sample, we do find it curious that the same trend is present (Silva, Novo, Prazeres, 1991).

Hence there appear to be important differences and questions waiting for an answer. The Rorschach normative study for the Portuguese population is being by Pires and his colleagues, and their results are awaited eagerly.

In the area of psychopathology, Silva and Prazeres administered the Rorschach and TAT to 25 men and women with bulbar duodenal ulcer. Ten of these patients were subsequently cured of their ulcer and 15 were not or had recurrences. Factor analysis of selected variables from each test revealed that the Rorschach could differentiate the cured and uncured groups, but the TAT did not (Silva & Prazeres, 1991). Rorschach results of this study were then examined by a step-by-step discriminant analysis and were presented at the Midwinter Meeting of the Society for Personality Assessment in Washington in 1992. A discriminant function was derived that correctly placed 92% of the subjects in their proper group.

Three other informational papers were presented by Silva at Portuguese scientific meetings in 1992: "Research Methodology and New Developments in the Rorschach Comprehensive System," which drew attention to the publication of the second edition of *The Rorschach: A Comprehensive System. Vol. 2* (1991); "Research with Projective Methods in Portugal During the Last Two Decades and Future Perspectives"; and "Psychoanalytic Theory and Projective Methods in Psychological Assessment of Children."

B. Gonçalves has continued his research on the Szondi test and published in 1991 a study identifying differential characteristics of the three schizophrenic groups he had studied previously. Using a discriminant analysis, he demonstrated that these groups differ clearly in their responses and internal consistency. He concluded that the test is able to identify three groups corresponding to three specific types of schizophrenics (Gonçalves, 1991).

At the University of Porto, Carneiro has followed up his research on graphic projective methods and published regularly on the Tree Test and the Family Test (Carneiro, 1986–1992), and Pires and Borges have published a study on the Rorschach normative data using a sample of suburban subjects in Porto (Pires & Borges, 1990).

Future Trends

Having presented this broad overview on the teaching, study, and research on projective methods in Portugal, we can say that much has been accomplished in these last two decades, and the most important of these has been finding a respected place in psychological practice and research. The teaching of projective methods has found much support and is expected to lead to post-graduate courses that will foster deeper and more consistent learning. The Portuguese Rorschach Society and the Personality Assessment Section will continue with their task of training and consolidation of knowledge outside the universities. Several studies are proceeding at a good pace, some of which are already in press for publication. Among them we wish to emphasize Pires' on the Rorschach Portuguese normative data according to Exner's criteria; Silva's Rorschach normative study for Lisbon children; M. Gonçalves' study of the relationship between self-report measures and the Rorschach test; Fernandes' study of projection in the Rorschach and the TAT; Moita's work on the Zulliger test; and Marques' studies of masculine and feminine expression in adolescence.

This report may have overlooked some details and studies. However, we think we have referred to most of our studies and initiatives, as well as Portuguese work published abroad. We might add that there are many new proposals blossoming in the Portuguese milieu. The future, we think, holds much promise.

Résumé

Ce travail commence par situer l'enseignement, la recherche et l'étude du Rorschach et d'autres méthodes projectives en liaison avec le chemin parcouru par la science psychologique au Portugal, au long de ce siècle. Après une courte période initiale qu'on pourrait considérer en quelque sorte favorable, la Psychologie a rencontré très tôt tout genre de barrières, d'opposition, de méfiance qui ont engendré un grand retard dans son développement par rapport à ce qui se passait dans la plupart des pays de l'Europe occidentale. La dictature au pouvoir, depuis la fin des annés vingt jusqu'à 1974, semble avoir toujours regardé de travres cette science et ne lui a jamais réservé un bon accueil. Bien que l'idée d'une licence en Psychologie à la Université de Lisbonne remonte aux annés 40, elle n'a vu sa concrétisation qu'après la chute du régime. Alors, chacune des trois Universités existantes a vu la naissance d'un cours supérieur de Psychologie, devenu Faculté de Psychologie en 1980. En dehors de l'Université, l'Institut Supérieur de Psychologie Appliquée (ISPA), né en 1962, a été le plus important centre d'enseignement de la Psychologie au Portugal.

Depuis l'article le plus ancien, daté de 1938, et se rapportant au Rorschach et à son importance dans la criminologie, la litérature concernant les méthodes projectives n'a cessé de paraître. En sont témoin les divers travaux que ont donné lieu à des thèses de licence au long de plusieurs décennies et les articles de revue, particulièrement consacrés aux tests graphiques qui ont connu un certain essor du fait que la Psychologie de l'enfant était le secteur le plus développé à cette époque.

Avec la naissance des cours supérieurs et des Facultés de Psychologie, l'enseignement de la méthodologie projective a conquis sa place tout en y ayant trouvé un bon accueil. _ l'ISPA, cet enseignement occupe un nombre élevé d'heures, en particulier l'aire de la Psychologie Clinique; dans les Facultés ce nombre est moins grand mais le sujet prend une place saillant dans les matières de diagnostic et d'évaluation de la personnalité.

La recherche s'est affermi à partir des annés 70 n'ayant cessé depuis lors de produire ses fruits et sous la forme de thèses de doctorat—cinc déjà discutés et cinc en élaboration—et sous la forme d'articles de revue ou de communications présentés dans des réunions nationales et internationales. Soulignons la varieté des tests étudiés: Rorschach, TAT, CAT, CAT-H, Zulliger, Szondi, test de l'Arbre et même la création d'une épreuve projective originellement portugaise, une épreuve dont les caractéristiques et les premiers résultats sont pleins de promesses.

L'élargissement des champs de l'évaluation et la possibilité de créer prochainement des études pos-graduées universitaires en méthodologie projective nous permettent de regarder l'avenir avec beaucoup de confiance.

Resumen

El presente trabajo comienza por situar la enseñanza, la investigatión y el estudio del Rorschach y otros métodos proyectivos en ligación con el camino penosamente recorrido por la ciencia de la Psicología en Portugal, a lo largo deste siglo. Después de comienzos auspiciosos, la Psicología vino a deparar con todo tipo de obstáculos, oposición, desconfianza que determinaron un importante retraso en su desarrollo, en comparación con lo que se hacia en la mayoria de los países en Europa ocidental. El regimén dictatorial en el poder, desde finales de la década de los años 20 hasta 1974, parece haber siempre mirado la Psicología de una manera de través y jamás le concedió acogida. No obstante la idea de una licenciatura en Psicología en la universidad de Lisboa haya sido expressa en el final de los años 40, solo después de la caída de aquel regimen se crearon, en las Universidades para entonces existentes, los respectivos cursos que se transformaron em 1980 en Faculdades. Fuera de la Universidad, el Instituto Superior de Psicología Aplicada (ISPA), que surgió en el año de 1962, constituyó el principal centro de enseñanza de la Psicologia.

La literatura referente à los métodos proyectivos, a partir del escrito conocido más antíguo en el año de 1938, que se refiere a Rorschach y a su importancia en el campo de la criminologia, tuvo una expresión continuada. Son testimonios de eso los variados trabajos que constituyeron tesis de licenciatura y doctorado desde los años 40 hasta los años 70, o los artículos de las revistas, con particular enfasis para los testes gráficos ya que la Psicología del niño fué el sector que mayor importancia alcanzó.

Con la creación de los cursos y de las faculdades de Psicología, la enseñanza de la metodologia proyectiva encontró una acogida receptiva. En el ISPA, es elevado el número de horas que le es dedicado, sobretodo en el área de la Psicologia Clínica; en las faculdades, ese número es inferior, pero el tema asume lugar de destaque en las matérias de diagnóstico y evaluación de la personalidad.

La investigación se afirmó a partir de los años 70, y no ha dejado de produzir sus frutos ya sea como tesis de doctorado—5 tesis discutidas y 5 en elaboratión—ya sea como en articulos de revistas, ponencias en reuniones nacionales e internacionales, dando testimonio de una actividad intensa en el campo. Es de destacar la diversidad de los tests estudiados: Rorschach, TAT, CAT, CAT-H, Zulliger, Szondi, test del Arbol y la propia creación de una prueba proyectiva para niños, "Era una vez . . . ," la primera genuínamente portuguesa, que se presenta de manera promisoria.

El futuro se nos presenta auspicioso, con la expansión de los campos de evaluación y con la posibilidad de una proxima creación de estudios universitários de pos-graduación en el area de los tests proyectivos.

Danilo Silva and Maria Emilia Marques

Resumo

O trabalho começa por situar o ensino, a investigação e o estudo do Rorschach e outros métodos projectivos em ligação com o caminho penosamente percorrido pela ciência psicológica em Portugal, ao longo deste século. Após um início auspicioso, a Psicologia veio a deparar com todo o tipo de obstáculos, oposição, desconfiança que determinaram um importante atraso no desenvolvimento, em comparação com o que se passava na maioria dos países da Europa Ocidental. A ditadura no poder, desde o começo da década de 30 até 1974, parece sempre ter olhado a Psicologia de soslaio e nunca a acolheu condignamente. Embora a ideia de uma licenciatura em Psicologia na Universidade de Lisboa tenha sido expressa já no final dos anos 40, só após a queda daquele regime vieram a criar-se, nas Universidades então existentes, os respectivos cursos superiores que se transformaram em Faculdades em 1980. Fora da Universidade, o Instituto Superior de Psicologia Aplicada (ISPA), surgido em 1962), constituiu o principal centro de ensino da Psicologia.

A literatura referente aos métodos projectivos manteve uma certa continuidade, desde a publicação do escrito conhecido mais antigo, publicado em 1938 e referente ao Rorschach e sua importância na criminologia. Mostram-no os diversos trabalhos que constituíram teses de licenciatura e de doutoramento, dos anos 40 aos anos 70, ou os artigos de revista, com particular destaque para os testes gráficos, já que a Psicologia da Criança foi o sector que maior importância alcançou.

Com a criação dos Cursos Superiores e, depois, das Faculdades de Psicologia, o ensino da metodologia projectiva teve acolhimento receptivo. No ISPA, é elevado o número de horas que lhe é dedicado, sobretudo na área da Psicologia Clínica; nas faculdades, esse número é inferior mas o tema assume lugar de destaque nas matérias de diagnóstico e de avaliação da personalidade.

A investigação afirmou-se a partir dos anos 70 e não deixou de produzir os seus frutos, quer sob a forma de teses de doutoramento—5 já discutidas e 5 em elaboração—quer sob a forma de artigos de revista, comunicações em reuniães nacionais e internacionais, dando testemunho de uma actividade intensa no campo. Destaque-se a diversidade dos temas estudados: Rorschach, TAT, CAT-A, CAT-H, Zulliger, Szondi, teste da ãrvore e até a criação de uma prova projectiva para crianças, "Era uma vez …," a primeira genuinamente portuguesa que se apresenta bastante promissora.

O futuro mostra-se auspicioso, tendo em consideração a expansão dos campos de avaliação da personalidade e a possibilidade da próxima criação de estudos universitários de pós-graduação no sector dos métodos projectivos.

References

Bairrão, J. B. (1964) Alguns aspectos Psico-Sociais da Motivação. *Bol. do Instituto de Orientação Profissional*, 4º série, pp. 93–243.

Carneiro, F. C. (1966) A Grafologia e o Conhecimento do Homem. Separata da Revista *Cenáculo*, Ano V, nº 19.

Carneiro, F. C. (1978) Application Clinique. In Renée Stora (Ed.) *Le Test de l'Arbre*, Paris, Presses Universitaires de France, pp. 49–70.

Carneiro, F. C. (1986) *Le Test de l'Arbre: Une Approche Dynamique*. Thèse de Doctorat d'Etat, Université de Paris VII. (3 volumes policopiados).

Carneiro, F. C. (1986) A Simbolização no Test do Desenho da Família. *Jornal de Psicologia*, 5, 13–17.

Carneiro, F. C. (1987) O Teste do Desenho da Arvore: Influência da Linguagem na Representação Gráfica. *Revista de Psicologia e de Ciências da Educação*, 2, 51–58.

Carneiro, F. C. (1987a) O Teste do Desenho da Árvore—A Relação Tronco/Coroa. *Jornal de Psicologia*, 6, 3–8.

Carneiro, F. C. (1988) O Desenho da Família de Adolescentes Psicóticos. *Jornal de Psicologia*, 7, 8–12.

Carneiro, F. C. (1990) O Teste de Escolha de Árvores. *Jornal de Psicologia*, 9, 3–7.

Carneiro, F. C. (1992) O Desenho das Três Árvores. *Jornal de Psicologia*, 10, 19–21.

Fagulha, T. P. (1992) *A Prova "Era uma vez … " Uma Prova Projectiva para Crianças.* Tese de Doutoramento, Lisboa, Faculdade de Psicologia e de Ciências da Educação.

Fernandes, I. B. (1977) Contribuição para uma Lista Portuguesa de Respostas Banais no Psicodiagnóstico de Rorschach. *Revista Portuguesa de Psicologia, VI*, (1), 285–303.

Fernandes, I. B. (1985) O Test de Apercepção Temática (TAT): Teoria e Método de V.Shentoub. Apresentação de seis narrativas. *Revista Portuguesa de Psicologia*, 22, 111–131.

Fernandes, I. B. (1989) O Funcionamento Narcísico e as Organizações Limite da Personalidade no Rorschach. *Caderno do Seminário Rorschach e Mecanismos de Defesa*, Lisboa, Secção de Avaliação da Personalidade/Sociedade Portuguesa de Psicologia, 50–67.

Fernandes, I. B. (1991) Estudo Comparativo da Projecção no Rorschach e no TAT com um Grupo de Sujeitos Esquizofrénicos. *Revista Portuguesa de Psicologia*, 27, 39–45.

Gonçalves, B. (1989) *La Schizophrénie à travers le Test de Szondi*. Tese de Doutoramento, Université Catholique de Louvain.

Gonçalves, B. (1989) A Esquizofrenia através do Teste de Szondi. *Revista Portuguesa de Psicologia, 25,* 7-29.

Gonçalves, B. (1991) As Respostas dos Esquizofrénicos ao Teste de Szondi: Estudo Tipológico. *Revista Portuguesa de Psicologia, 27,* 75-84.

Marques, M. E. (1991) L'Adolescence comme Processus de Transgression des Limites: son Expression au Féminin et au Masculin. *Rorschachiana, XVII,* 308-312.

Marques. M. E. (1991a) As Manifestaçães dos Mecanismos Adaptativo-Defensivos nos Rorschach de Adolescentes. *Análise Psicológica,* série IX, 2, 203-290.

Marques. M. E. (1991b) A Transcrição no Rorschach das Expressões Masculina e Feminina na Pré-adolescência e Adolescência. *Actas de Psicologia Clínica,* 171-181.

Marques. M. E. (1991c) As Particulariedades do Funcionamento Psicológico dos Pré-Adolescentes e Adolescentes, nas Expressões Masculina e Feminina através do Rorschach. *Actas de Psicologia Clínica,* pp. 171-181. S.P.P.C., Ed. Cosmos, Lisboa.

Moita, V. (1981/82) *Modalités de Réponses au Rorschach et Statut Sociométrique chez les Pré-Adolescents: Contribuition à l'Étude de la Personnalité du Garçon Pubère.* Université Paris V, René Descartes (policopiado).

Moita, V. (1983) A Angústia como Conceito Operatório na Técnica Projectiva de Rorschach. *Análise Psicológica, 1,* 5-16.

Moita, V. (1988) Contributos para a determinação do índice de angústia através da técnica Rorschach. (A publicar na Revista de Psicologia e de Ciências da Educação. Fac. de Psic. e de C. da Educ. da Universidade do Porto).

Novo, R. (1988) *A Dependência-Independência do Campo e o Rorschach.* Faculdade de Psicologia e de Ciências da Educação, Lisboa.

Novo, R. (1991) A Dependência-Independência do Campo e o Rorschach: Estudo de Dois Grupos de Estudantes Universitários. *Revista Portuguesa de Psicologia, 27,* 29-38.

Pina, L. (1938) O Psicodiagnóstico de Rorschach em Criminologia. *Separata do Boletim dos Institutos de Criminologia,* 1-29.

Pires, A. A. (1986) O Teste de Rorschach: Alguns Aspectos Relacionados com as Críticas e as Novas Perspectivas de Utilização. *Jornal de Psicologia, 5* 8-13.

Pires, A. A. (1987)) *O Teste de Rorschach na Avaliação Psicológica: Fundamentação, Validade e Estudo Normativo na População Portuguesa.* Faculdade de Psicologia e de Ciências da Educação, Porto.

Pires, A. A. e Borges, M. I. P. (1990) Estudo Normativo do Teste de Rorschach na População Portuguesa: A Região do Grande Porto. *Jornal de Psicologia, 9,* 12-16.

Silva, D. R. (1968/69) O Método Aperceptivo-Temático de Avaliação de Motivos. O Motivo de Realização. *Bol. do Instituto de Orientação Profissional,* 4e série, 3-124.

Silva, D. R. (1971) A Perspectiva Psicanalítica de Interpretação do TAT. Monografia nº 5, Separata da *Revista da Faculdade de Letras,* III série, *14,* 138 páginas, Lisboa.

Silva, D. R. (1975/76) A Estrutura da Personalidade através do Rorschach e do TAT. *Revista Portuguesa de Psicologia, 12/13,* 31-45.

Silva, D. R. (1982) *O Teste de Apercepção para Crianças (Figuras Humanas)–CAT-H: Estudo de Normas*. Lisboa, edição do Instituto Nacional de Investigação Científica.

Silva, D. R. (1980/81/82) Análise dos Estudos sobre a Validade do Rorschach em Psicologia Clínica. *Revista Portuguesa de Psicologia, 17/18/19*, 73–118.

Silva, D. R. (1983/84) Algumas Características de Resposta de Rapazes e Raparigas ao CAT-H. *Revista Portuguesa de Psicologia, 20/21*, 7–34.

Silva, D. R. (1985) O TAT: Algumas Questões Teóricas e Perspectivas da sua Utilização. *Revista Portuguesa de Psicologia, 22*, 101–109.

Silva, D. R. (1986) Exner e a Reposição do Teste de Rorschach. *Revista Portuguesa de Pedagogia, XX*, 135–168.

Silva, D. R. (1986) O Sistema Integrativo do Rorschach de John E. Exner, Jr.. *Revista Portuguesa de Psicologia, 23*, 189–238.

Silva, D. R. (1987/88) Um Estudo da Consistência Temporal no Rorschach. *Revista Portuguesa de Psicologia, 24*, 159–170.

Silva, D. R. (1989) Questões sobre o Rorschach de Dois Grupos de Crianças Portuguesas no Termo do 1º Ano de Escolaridade. *Revista Portuguesa de Psicologia, 25*, 45–57.

Silva, D. R. (1991) Análise do Rorschach de Três Grupos de Crianças Portuguesas no Termo do 1º Ano de Escolaridade. *Revista Portuguesa de Psicologia, 27*, 61–73.

Silva, D. R., Prazeres, N. (1991) Estudo Comparativo do Rorschach e do TAT de Dois Grupos de Sujeitos com um Diagnóstico de Ulcera Duodenal. *Revista Portuguesa de Psicologia, 27*, 61–73. Publicado em língua francesa em *Rorschachiana, XVII*, 188–194.

Silva, D. R., Novo, R., Prazeres, N. (1991) Serão os Dados Normativos do Rorschach Apresentados por Exner Válidos para a População Europeia? Ensaio com uma Amostra Portuguesa. *Revista Portuguesa de Psicologia, 27*, 13–27. Publicado também na *Revista de la Sociedad Española del Rorschach y Métodos Proyectivos*, 1990, *3*, 33–40.

Silva, D. R., Novo, R., Prazeres, N. (1992) Diferenças entre Crianças Portuguesas e Americanas em Algumas Variáveis do Rorschach: Uma Questão Transcultural. *Revista Portuguesa de Psicologia, 28*, 149–162.

Family Changing Process: Integration of Two Modalities of Rorschach Test Administration

Concepcion Sendin

Hospital Psiquiatrico de Leganes & Universidad Complutense, Madrid, Spain

Carmen Garcia Alba

Hospital Psiquiatrico de Leganes, Madrid, Spain

Beginning in 1960, several authors became interested in the possibility of using the Rorschach method to study communication and interactive processes in groups, families, and couples. Blanchard (1959) introduced the Consensus Rorschach, which subsequently was extended to various lines of research with families. Loveland, Wynne, and Singer (1963), for example, used a similar consensus method that they called the Family Rorschach. Bauman and Roman (1964) developed a consensus method that they defined as Interaction Testing.

Following the work of these authors, application of the Rorschach as an exceptionally good instrument for live observation of group interactions became complex and diversified, involving numerous different methods and many subtle nuances in the administration of the method and the interpretation of the data. However, common to all the variations of the Consensus Rorschach that have emerged has been a central interest in studying the processes of human communication. Every variation that has been used consists basically of asking the group, family, or couple to examine the blots and look for answers on which they can all agree (that is, reach consensus). Examiners then study the verbal and non-verbal behaviors elicited by each card, as well as the individual roles, attitudes, and the like that appear in the course of the solving-problem task. In this way, the Rorschach method became introduced into a field of research that historically had not been anticipated, but that seems at

47

present to be offering considerable opportunity for useful application of the method.

Without attempting to provide a complete bibliography of the work that has been done with the consensus approach, we would like to mention the contributions of some authors whose publications have been especially influential in this area. Willi (1978) proposed three "interactional variables" for the interpretation of Consensus Rorschach data:

1. Hierarchies in the handling of the cards—number of contributions by the members, their influence on decisions, their assertiveness, etc.
2. Style of affective relating—opinions given about each other's answers, nature of overall group communication, emotional similarity and complementarity among members, etc.
3. Cooperation—number of common solutions, quality of the responses, quality of the decisions, etc.

To evaluate each of these aspects, Willi used numerous categories of the following type: the order in which the members handle the cards; who is assuming responsibility for deciding on a response; evidence of rivalry or tension in the group; ways in which leadership is shown; indications of creativity or rigidity; inattention to the task, passivity, or lack of critical consideration; how roles are distributed among members; and the cohesiveness of communication. Willi concludes, "The examination of a group by means of the Rorschach seems to polarize much better than any other method the roles of each member of the system" (p. 280).

Magni, Ferruzza, and Barison (1982), applying the Rorschach to couples, utilized for their analysis of subject interpretations the concepts of "symmetry and complementarity" introduced by Bateson (1936) and the idea of "Relational Control" introduced by Haley (1963). They defined levels of analysis for evaluating these notions, based on modalities of human communication described by Schefflen (1973): (a) linguistic modalities, which involve language and (b) corporal modalities, which involve forms of bodily posture, movement, feeling, and action. They then subdivided these categories into smaller units of analysis to facilitate their evaluation and mentioned a series of items that allowed them to achieve an improved blend of the interpretive data, including lexical and verbal form, contents, information, roles, behaviors, and types of communication.

Sokolova (1985) also made important contributions to the use of the Rorschach Method in studying the structure and dynamics of family interaction. She stressed the particular utility of the Rorschach in diagnosing disorder of communication: "This test combines the possibilities of the traditional version (oriented toward the intrapsychic life of the individual) and the perspective of studying the structure and dynamics of reciprocal interpersonal interactions in a family" (p. 146).

Comparing the Rorschach with other methods used for interplay measurement, Sokolova concludes as follows:

> Unlike other methods, in which it is necessary to arrive conjointly at one decision or clearly defined result, in Rorschach all the solutions of the participants (their interpretation of the cards) have equal status, and, consequently, divergence among them is almost inevitable. Under these conditions, the process of seeking a common solution, the interchange of opinions about the inkblots, will tend to reveal not only preferences concerning what "objective" contents to report but also the reciprocal emotional attitudes of each member of the family system. Thus the "consensus process" provides us an opportunity to observe quite directly styles of interpersonal cooperation (p. 146).

Sokolova also notes that, with respect to methodology, the basic problem with this modality of administering the Rorschach is that so far neither a single procedure, nor a single way of treating the results, nor a single conceptual framework has been achieved. Instead, professionals have had much difficulty arriving at their own consensus regarding each of these.

Pes, Parisi, Giovanell, and Cherubini (1987) have also worked with the Rorschach in group settings. They integrate classical interpretation of the test with the theoretical principles of the relational-systemic approach, and they discuss the diagnostic and prognostic utility, from their point of view, of converting the method into an "interactive stimulus" for the group being studied. Finally, we wish to cite the work of Nakamura and Nakamura (1987), who, as the previous authors, noted possible use of the Rorschach for direct observation of communication processes. They added the variation of selecting only five of the 10 cards, in order to simplify the examination. Nakamura and Nakamura justify this variation on the basis of their data, saying that the information they obtained using Cards I, II, IV, VII, and X is essentially the same as with the full set of cards.

Another novel approach of this Japanese group that seems interesting was using the Rorschach method not just as a diagnostic tool, but also essentially as a therapeutic intervention with the family system. What they do is film the testing session as they might any other, and then play back the tape to the family and discuss with them the interactive processes that have emerged. This feedback session plays an essential role in the future course of treatment.

After a full review (here we have given an account of only basic authors, and there is a very extensive bibliography on this subject), we considered the possibility of using the Rorschach with this approach in our daily practice with families, in order to observe more directly the interactive processes. We decided to use the method proposed by Nakamura and Nakamura, because it has two features that are well-suited to the pace of our work: (a) simplicity of administration and (b) the possibility of using the diagnostic session as a feedback session in the treatment.

As prescribed by their method, the Rorschach is administered to the entire family in two phases, a Consensus Process and an Image Process.

1. *Family Consensus Process*. In this phase all members are asked to look at each card, to discuss their individual answers, and then to reach agreement on one of them, so that they give the examiner only one consensus response for each card.

Throughout each of these solving-problem tasks, it is possible to observe the relational style of the family with the examiner, with the stimuli, and with each other, under the stress-inducing circumstances of having to make their decisions. Likewise, by comparing their ways of dealing with the different situations posed by each card, it is possible to evaluate how rigid or flexible a family's patterns are. The analysis of the data focuses on the following variables: who takes each card; whether the card is passed from one family member to another; who gives the first answer and what the quality of this answer is; how the discussion process flows, what kind of consensus responses they give, and how much spontaneous discussion emerges among the members of the group; which responses given by whom are accepted by the family as their consensus responses; which family member takes charge of the process and does this change or remain the same for one card to the next; who talks first to the examiner when tension in the group increases; what changes occur in the family dynamics from card to card; and which family members are systematically excluded from the discussion.

2. *Family Image Process*. In this phase the examiner places before the family the five cards used in the previous phase and asks them to choose the one that, for each of them, best represents their image of each member of the group. They are also asked to explain why they made this choice.

In this phase, the basic interpretative considerations involve (a) the exploration by means of the expressed images of how members of the

50

family perceive each other; (b) the evaluation of capacity for mutual empathy; (c) the comparison of the chosen images with the consensus response given to each card in the previous phase; (d) the facilitation, through an active stance on the part of the examiner of interchange among family members; (e) the changes in the roles attitudes of each family member, as compared to the consensus phase; and (f) the observation of family responsiveness as an important prognostic factor in the subsequent therapeutic intervention.

We would not want to omit mentioning that some Rorschachers may perhaps be surprised to learn of this use of the test, as we were ourselves. It is appropriate to explain that this modality does not eliminate traditional use of the Rorschach. To the contrary, it complements and enhances it, offering an interesting avenue for research and clinical practice that, at least in our country, has been almost unknown up to the present time.

In support of this modality, we present here a case study involving the results of a Rorschach individually administered to a 10-year-old girl during the process of evaluation and complemented with a family Rorschach that we decided to use because of the severity of the case. To evaluate the process of change, we also present individual and family Rorschachs that were taken one year later.

Procedure

The family with which we worked included four members: Father, a 43-year-old carpenter with an elementary school education; Mother, age 37, with an elementary school education and working as a cleaning lady in a hospital; Almudena, 13 years old and in her first year of high school; and Cristina, age 10 and in the sixth grade. The family was referred to our Mental Health Center by a psychiatrist at the hospital where the mother works, with a request for psychological evaluation of Cristina in connection with suspicion of schizophrenia.

We conducted an individual diagnostic evaluation of Cristina using interviews, drawings, a Raven, and the Rorschach. The results confirmed the presence of serious perceptual-cognitive disorders that could easily be seen as consistent with the diagnosis suspected by the psychiatrist. When this information was relayed to him, he decided to discard the possibility of neurological disorder which he had originally considered and for which the results were negative. Anticipating that long-term treatment would be needed, he turned the case over to us with a recommendation for a combined pharmacologic and psychotherapeutic approach (with strong emphasis on the pharmacologic).

Christina's behavior at this time was very strange and maladaptive, both at home and in school. During class sessions she would climb up on the tables in the room and jump from one to another; on occasion she would imitate her teacher's gestures or suddenly take off her underwear; she insisted on traveling in the luggage compartment in the family car; she would say that she was "Princess Sarah," and so forth.

In spite of all this, the presenting complaint of the family was Cristina's "disobedience and poor school performance." This was the chief concern expressed first to the referring psychiatrist and subsequently to us when they came to our center. The parents suspected intellectual limitations in Cristina and hoped that these would subside with the passage of time. The general developmental history of this girl was not remarkable, except for occasional nocturnal enuresis until age 6 or 7 and apparently chronic poor appetite. On the other hand, her disturbed conduct, her bizarre ideas, and her anxiety and difficulties sustaining effort had always been present, according to the parents, but were seen by them as "normal things in a little girl" and had not previously led them to seek any help. On taking over the case, we initially decided to defer pharmacologic treatment until we had a better understanding of the family dynamics. This was explained to parents, along with a proposal for an approach involving the whole family and including the Rorschach.

Accordingly, we worked with the entire family for about 15 months. This is the period that we describe in this communication, and it preceded a current treatment phase in which we are coordinating our work with the psychological team at Cristina's school. During the first 15 months we proceeded in several stages:

1. Individual assessment of Cristina in response to the psychiatric referral.

2. Assuming responsibility for the case and proposing a family approach. At this point one of the difficulties was the discrepancy between the family's expectations (medication as stressed by the psychiatrist) and our proposal (first understanding the family dynamics). This discrepancy was manifested, among other things, by the family at first missing sessions or the father not coming, even though we had made it clear that the appointments were for all of them.

3. The family assessment, including a family Rorschach administered according to the method proposed by Nakamura and Nakamura.
4. Sharing the results with the family and proposing family treatment, which they finally accepted without unusual difficulty.
5. Re-administration of both the individual and family Rorschach one year later to evaluate change.

Results

Comparison of the Individual Rorschachs

Table 1 shows several interesting changes from the first to the second testing in Cristina's individual Rorschach.

Table 1. Individual Rorschach comparison.

1. Variables with changes	First Rorschach	Second Rorschach
R	34	15
SCZI	6	4
Adj D	+3	0
EB	10:4.5	3:4
FC	0	2
Pure C	1	0
Zd	−19.5	−6.0
P	11	6
Sum H	19	5
MOR	2	3
FAB	3	0
Fd	2	0
An	3	0
2. Variable without changes	First Rorschach	Second Rorschach
Afr	.31	.36
Sum T	0	0

Initially it seemed that her case was going to be difficult to modify, because her disorder showed such strong features of stability and rigidity. Indeed, in spite of the greater constriction observed in the second Rorschach (lower R, more emotional control, fewer bizarre verbaliza-

53

tions), the SCZI is still elevated at 4. Even so, the SCZI has gone down by two points, from 6 to 4, and there is a good possibility that the perceptual-cognitive disorders of this girl may not be of a schizophrenic type. This finding leads us to think that, although in adults the SCZI has achieved considerable precision and produces few false positives (Exner, 1990), in children it may not happen in the same way. At least with respect to Cristina, the SCZI has been modified in a case of supposed chronicity.

In view of the much greater productivity in the first Rorschach (elevated R), the changes in variables with low values should be interpreted cautiously. These changes could be influenced by the change in R.

The observed changes in use of resources may be produced by a decrease in deliberate ideation (from 10 M down to 3 M). Although this could be seen as a negative finding, Cristina on the second testing is using less M (quantitative decrease) but is doing so in a more adaptive way (qualitative improvement). In the second Rorschach M disappeared, and the percentage of Mo increased from 20% (first testing) to 33% (second testing). The decrease in Popular responses is related to these changes in M, because 5 of the P in the first Rorschach occurred in conjunction with poor quality M responses.

The changes in Cristina's style of processing information (Zd decrease from –19.5 to –6) are important in explaining some changes observed in her conduct. She continues in the second Rorschach to show tendencies to give short, rapid answers, without carefully examining a stimulus field, but there was clear improvement in her capacity to keep her attention focused on environmental clues, a capacity that obviously contributed to adaptive behavior.

In regard to interpersonal relations, she has changed her perception of human figures by showing on the second Rorschach fewer imaginary percepts of people (the (H) decreased from 10 to 2). There appears to be a slight increase in pessimistic thinking from the first to the second test (MOR goes from 2 to 3), but feelings of personal devaluation have disappeared from her record (V = 0). Perhaps some previous emotional discomfort has shifted over to the ideational domain.

Features of dependency and tendencies to establish bizarre relationships between objects and events, present in the first Rorschach (Fd = 2, P = 11, FAB = 3), disappear in the second Rorschach. This is also likely to provide a basis for change in her interpersonal functioning.

Although we do not have sufficient data to confirm it, it seems interesting to formulate a hypothesis about the lack of body concern in the second testing compared to heightened concern in the first (An+Xy goes from 3 to 0). Let us remember that, at the beginning, the family as well as the psychiatrist thought that Cristina had an organic disorder. This belief was reflected in her first Rorschach by such answers as "A brain that bleeds a lot" (Card II). The absence of Anatomy responses in the second testing could have resulted from clarification of this matter during the treatment.

In contrast to these several variables that showed change, we need to mention two variables that are unchanged from the first to the second testing. The Affective Ratio is essentially the same in both records (from .31 to .36). Christina retains a low affective responsiveness and avoidance of emotionally charged situations, which identifies risk of social isolation, given her age, and at the same time reinforces her control systems.

The second unchanged variable, closely related to the first, involves her failure to use texture (T = 0 in both records). It appears that this girl does not reach out for close relationships with others and may experience close contact as an invasion of her personal space. Together with her low Affective Ratio, this absence of texture increases her risk of being emotionally isolated. The persistence of these two variables without variation identify a priority in planning future intervention. They tell us that it will be necessary to work on the theme of her affective relationships in order to alleviate as much as possible her strong inclination toward emotional isolation.

Comparison of the Family Rorschachs

With respect to the Consensus phase of the family Rorschach, Table 2 shows some interesting changes on the second testing.

Compared to the first family Rorschach, the second one reflects better perceptual accuracy accompanied by the disappearance of thinking disorder (X+% is up; P is up; FAB = 0). There is a higher level of cognitive work with better adaptation to reality (Mo is up, DQ+ is up). Egocentricity changes qualitatively, with the more narcissistic elements disappearing (Fr = 0; (2) is better). At the same time there appears to be an increase in the passivity and conventionality of this family (P is up; Mp is up).

This last point raises a deeper question, because in both the individual and the family records we observed that improvements in perceptual and ideational functioning (which were corroborated in Christina's

Table 2. Family Rorschach comparison.

1. *Consensus Phase*	First Rorschach	Second Rorschach
Card I	Bat	Bat
Card II	A reflected bird	Two rabbits
Card IV	Women grasping a giant	Giant sitting on a stump
Card VII	Head of a but	Two Indians sitting down
Card X	A flower	A forest with flowers

2. *Image Phase*	First Rorschach	Second Rorschach
Father (F)	Card IV (All)	Card IV (All)
Mother (M)	Card I (M,F,A)	Card X (M,C)
	Card VII (C)	Card II (F)
		Card VII (A)
Almudena (A)	Card VII (F,M,C)	Card X (F)
	Card II (A)	Card I (M,C)
		Card II (A)
Christina (C)	Card X (All)	Card I (F)
		Card II (A)
		Card VII (M,C)

manifest conduct) had been accompanied by increased constriction and conventionality. This would lead us to question the rationale for treatments considered "successful," because typically only the adaptive improvements in subjects are mentioned, without considering losses in their individuality that may also have occurred.

As for the image phase, Table 2 indicates in the first place an increased opportunity for divergent opinions to be expressed in the family. In the first testing the selection criteria are much more unanimous and are produced almost without discussion. In contrast, in the second testing there is much more opportunity for interchange and for family members to maintain their individual opinions.

Regarding the images chosen by each of the family members, note that only the father selects the same image on both protocols—seeing Card IV (first the "Women grasping a giant"; second the "Giant sitting on a stump") as representing all four family members on both occasions. Cristina's images change the most, becoming perceived in a more conventional and adaptive way, but without explicit emotional aspects (the Card X "Flower" for all family members on the first testing; the images of "Bat," "Two rabbits," and "Two Indians sitting down""on the second). In some way the family seems to capture, in the images perceived by

Cristina, what we pointed out in our questioning of the cost-benefit of her treatment: namely, that at least in this case the adaptive improvements are accompanied by a constriction of more idiographic features.

Finally, let us examine changes observed in the family interaction. The greatest richness of nuances and, at the same time, the most difficult to communicate in a few words, involve the changes observed in the video-tapes obtained with this family.

The first family Rorschach was characterized by communication involving a very constricted interaction with very little spontaneous conversation, fear of disagreement, and great difficulty on the part of the examiner in understanding the process that was leading to consensus. Cristina's opinions were systematically excluded, without correction of her inadequate perceptions, and there was a clear alliance between the father and the older sister, Almudena, who imposed their opinions on the others. The mother seemed vague and uncertain and played a very secondary role.

In the second family Rorschach there was a quantitative and qualitative change in their interactions, in that the responses were more shared and discussed. No one was regularly excluded, the parental system appeared reinforced, and there were no clear alliances between any two family members.

In summary, we would like to cite Nakamura and Nakamura (1987, pp. 140–141), who provide a very clear description of peculiarities in communication in families with a schizophrenic member, compared with nonpatient families, and their manifestation in a family Rorschach. In families with a schizophrenic member, they observe that (a) the verbal interaction is much more limited; (b) the cards pass many fewer times from one family member to another; (c) there are fewer proposed responses and less spontaneous talking, so that the consensus response emerges suddenly, without sufficient discussion among the members; (d) the emotional atmosphere during the discussion is constricted and defensive; (e) there is little communication between the parents, who tend to form alliances with on of the children or to communicate with each other through the children; and (f) there is a tendency to keep rigidly to the same behavioral pattern throughout the whole process.

The style of communication in Cristina's family was almost identical to this pattern in the first Rorschach, but, as we have noted, was notably modified in the second Rorschach.

Conclusions

The first important conclusion that emerges from these results concerns the demonstrated usefulness and richness offered by the Rorschach method in this example of assessment and treatment planning, together with the enhancement of the method by the complementary data derived from the double administration, individual and family. It may be possible, as often mentioned in discussions of the amount of time devoted to a diagnostic process, that the necessary information could be obtained during the course of treatment. Nevertheless, what can be observed in one or two sessions with the technique described here, offers much more informed evaluation and increases the confidence the examiner can feel about it.

Moreover, we have observed that, at least in this case, the family Rorschach by itself fostered the process of change, facilitating group insight and action, along the lines suggested by Pes (1987), as an interactive stimulus. In this way, the visual images (video) of their own process appear to provide useful support for discussion of certain issues in the feedback sessions. Finally, we believe that this type of investigation needs to be extended to other families whose interactions are difficult to assess, in order to be able to compare the results and achieve cross-validation of the method.

Résumé

Nous presentons à ce travail un étude sur le processus de change dans une famille avec un membre psychotique, observé à travers de deux modalités d°administration du Rorschach: individuelle et familiale.

Après une ample revision bibliographique (nécessairement schématique dans cette exposition), nous décidons utiliser la modalité proposée par Nakamura et Nakamura (1987) pour l'application familiale, parce qu'elle presentait les avantages de simplicité et d'integration comme "session feedback" dans le processus therapeutique. Pour l'administration individuelle, nous suivons les critères du Système Comprehensive (Exner, dès 1972 à 1990).

Nous offrons ici les resultats des deux modalités d'application du Rorschach, ainsi comme la comparaison des données obtenus au diagnostique initial et au retest, aprés un année de traitement. Dans l'une et l'autre occasion on y a appliqué le Rorschach individuellemente (au membre psychotique) et groupellement (a tout le noyau familiel).

Nous postulons que ces deux modalités d'administration de l'epreuve ne sont pas excluants, mais absolument complementaires, parce qu'elles offrent diverses niveaux d'information, qui agrandissent et enrichissent la compréhension du cas. Des changes produits sont observables à travers des variables quantitatives et interactionales qui offrent une grande gamme de nuances quand on les utilise tout ensemble.

Nous attendons de pouvoir continuer avec ce tipe d'études pour aider à obtenir un mieux accord methodologique et pour utiliser avec majeure securité cette integration des differents tipes d'application du Rorschach. Nous croyons qu'elle peut être de grand utilité dans familles dont l'abordage est très difficile, parce qu'elle permet, avec un grand épargne de temps, diversifier des sources d'obtention de l'information.

Resumen

Presentamos en este trabajo un estudio sobre el proceso de cambio de una familia con un miembro psicótico, observado a través de dos modalidades de aplicación del Test de Rorschach: individual y familiar.

Tras una amplia revisión bibliográfica (necesariamente esquemática en esta exposición), decidimos utilizar la modalidad propuesta por Nakamura y Nakamura (1987) para la aplicación familiar, por presentar las ventajas de simplicidad e integración como "sesión feedback" en el proceso terapéutico. En la aplicación individual seguimos los criterios del Sistema Comprehensivo (Exner, de 1972 a 1990).

Ofrecemos los resultados de las dos modalidades de aplicación de la prueba de Rorschach, así como la comparación de los datos obtenidos en el diagnóstico inicial y en el retest después de un año de tratamiento. En ambas ocasiones se aplicó el Test de Rorschach individualmente (al miembro psicótico) y grupalmente (a todo el núcleo familiar).

Postulamos que ambas modalidades de administración de la prueba no son excluyentes, sino totalmente complementarias, ofreciendo cada una distintos niveles de información que amplían y enriquecen la comprensión del caso. Los cambios producidos son observables a través del análisis de variables cuantitativas e interaccionales, que proporcionan una gran gama de matices al ser utilizadas conjuntamente.

Esperamos poder continuar este tipo de estudios para ayudar a conseguir un mayor acuerdo metodológico yutilizar con mayor seguridad esta integración de tipos diferentes de aplicación del Test de Rorschach. Creemos que puede ser de gran utilidad en familias cuyo abordaje resulta dificil, ya que permite, con un gran ahorro de tiempo, diversificar las fuentes de obtención de la información.

References

Blanchard, W. (1959). The group process in gang rape. *Journal of Social Psychology, 49,* 159–266.

Blanchard, W. (1968). The Consensus Rorschach: Background and development. *Journal of Personality Assessment, 32,* 327–330.

Bauman, G., & Roman, M. (1964). Interaction testing ink the study of marital dominance. *Family Process, 3,* 230–242.

Exner, J. E. (1986). *The Rorschach: A comprehensive system.* Volume 1. *Basic Foundations* (2nd ed.). New York: Wiley.

Exner, J. E. (1990). *Alumni newsletter.* Asheville, NC: Rorschach Workshops.

Loveland, N., Wynne, L., & Singer, M. (1963). The Family Rorschach: A new method for studying family interaction. *Family Process, 2,* 187–215.

Magni, G., Ferruzza, E., & Barison, F. (1982). A preliminary report on the use of a new method of presenting the rorschach Test to evaluate the relationships of couples. *Journal of Family Therapy, 4,* 73–91.

Nakamura, S., & Nakamura, N. (1987). The Family Rorschach Technique. *Rorschachiana, 16,* 136–141.

Parisi, S., Pes, P., Giovanelli, G., & Cherubini, A. (1987). The Systemic Rorschach and group analysis. *Rorschachiana, 16,* 248.

Pes, P., Parisi, S., Giovanelli, G., & Cherubini, A. (1987). The System Rorschach. *Rorschachiana, 16,* 247.

Sokolova, Y. (1985). Modification del test de Rorschach para el diagnostico de la communicacion familiar. (Translated from Russian). *Voprosy Psikhlogii, 4,* 145–150.

Willi, J. (1978). The Rorschach as a test of direct interaction in groups. *Bulletin de Psychologie, 32,* 279–282.

Object Relations Theory and the Integration of Empirical and Psychoanalytic Approaches to Rorschach Interpretation

Bruce L. Smith

Berkeley, CA, USA

There have been two main traditions in clinical Rorschach psychology in the United States: the empirical and the psychoanalytic. Until recently, these have developed along parallel courses with little or no intersection. The empirical approach was largely dormant and ridiculed by academic psychology until the landmark work of John Exner and his collaborators (Exner, 1986) demonstrated the power of the Rorschach as an empirical instrument. By contrast, the psychoanalytic approach was in ascendance in clinical circles from the time of the pioneering work of Rapaport and his group (Rapaport, 1952; Rapaport, Gill, & Schafer, 1968; Schafer, 1948; Schafer, 1954) through the 1970s. More recently, the influence of object relations theory (Kissen, 1986; Kwawer, Lerner, Lerner, & Sugarman, 1980; Lerner & Lerner, 1988; Lerner, 1991) has re-kindled interest in a psychoanalytic approach to Rorschach testing.

Although there were early attempts to integrate these two approaches—either by attempting quantitative assessments of psychoanalytic constructs or by offering analytic interpretations of empirically-derived structural hypotheses, in general these two approaches have been seen as mutually inconsistent and even antagonistic. Indeed, the long debate between the empiricists and the psychoanalysts in assessment is part of a larger discussion termed by Bertrand Russell as the battle between the "narrow-minded" and the "fuzzy-headed." Despite the considerable heat generated, these discussions have largely missed the mark, because of a failure to recognize that rather than two different methods of assessment, what was being discussed were actually two different epistemologies. Whereas empirical methods of personality assessment represent the application of logical positivism to the field of psychodiagnostics—that is the prediction of future behavior—the psychoanalytic tradition is more rooted in hermeneutics, the science of signs and symbols and the generation of meaning (Ricoeur, 1970). It is not so much that empirical or analytic methods are better for answering psychodiagnostic questions, it is more that they provide different kinds of answers to different kinds of questions.

Epistemological Differences and Assessment Approaches

The philosophical differences mentioned above reflect a longstanding debate about scientific approaches to psychology and psychoanalysis. The psychoanalytic approach seeks to interpret the meaning of a particular phenomenon for the individual. Criteria for the adequacy of an interpretation include internal coherence, external coherence (that is, consistency with known facts about the individual or psychology in general), and the degree to which a particular interpretation leads to new revelations or further interpretive efforts. As such these interpretations are frequently neither falsifiable nor replicable, as they occur in a unique interpersonal or intersubjective context. Schwartz and Lazar (1979) discussed this point in its relationship to the Rorschach by asserting that the concept of probability when applied to Rorschach interpretations referred not to the frequency of the relationship between a response and a predicted event in the universe of similar responses, but to the confidence with which the interpreter makes the particular connection. As such they recognize the indivisibility of the interpreter-interpretation dyad. Because the likelihood of a particular response being given in precisely the same way in precisely the same context is nil, the approach to interpretation is unique for each individual subject. By contrast, a positivist approach seeks to define the individual in terms of communalities. Responses or clusters of responses are reduced to factors that can be compared across groups of individuals. The propositions generated are falsifiable and replicable.

Clearly, an empirical approach is necessary in most research contexts. Indeed, even psychoanalytic research with the Rorschach typically adopts a positivist methodology in which responses or protocols are encoded in terms that can be compared across groups of subjects independent of the specific examiner-examinee relationship. The work of

Blatt's and Mayman's groups are excellent examples of this (Blatt & Lerner, 1982; Cooper & Arnow, 1986; Mayman, 1967).

In the forensic arena, where predictions of future dangerousness or the evaluation of a defendant against some object standard are required, an approach which does not depend upon the subjective evaluation of the examiner is necessary. Similarly, there are clinical situations and questions that require an empirical approach, especially where the patient is not well known, or the treatment recommendations involve more than psychoanalytic psychotherapy.

While the empirical or positivist approach has the advantage of replicability and the articulation of objective standards, it specifically must omit certain classes of data. Psychoanalysis has a long tradition of utilizing subjective modes of data gathering. Referred to variously as the empathic mode (Kohut, 1971), the intersubjective approach (Stolorow, Brandchaft, & Atwood, 1987), or the therapeutic use of countertransference (Smith, 1990), this approach treats the therapist's or examiner's emotional experience in the therapeutic or testing situation as a source of information about the patient, assuming that it represents a mode of interpersonal communication. By definition, these data are not replicable, because they are unique to the particular examiner-examinee dyad. Indeed, it is assumed that the interpersonal meaning generated in a particular relationship will not necessarily be the same as that generated with a different examiner. This approach places great demands on the examiner, of course, because it necessitates the recognition of his or her stimulus value to the patient and its precipitation out before interpreting the patient's interpersonal communication. Nevertheless, Arnow and Cooper (Arnow & Cooper, 1988) and Lerner (Lerner, 1991), among others, have demonstrated the effectiveness of utilizing these subjective data in interpreting such phenomena as the use of projective identification or the reliance on self-objects.

Sequences of content, subtle nuances of language, and the relationship between content and formal properties of individual responses are other kinds of data that do not lend themselves to a positivist approach, not because they are necessarily subjective, but because they are likely to be unique, complex events that cannot be compared across subjects. For example, if a male subject gives the response of "two mean-looking women, staring intently" to Card VII and follows it up with "a cave with thick walls and a small opening" to the central white space, we might interpret that he is projecting a malevolent maternal introject into the blot and that the second response reflects a flight into a safe haven away from the

63

threat. At a deeper level, we might even consider the second response as reflecting an unconscious fantasy of a return to the womb in the face of adult sexuality. Interpretations such as these are made on the basis of a careful analysis of the precise wording of the Rorschach record. In formulating such an hypothesis, the clinician moves back and forth among the content, the formal properties (in this case the location of the responses) and the patient's language. The resulting formulation is in not the form of a statement about traits or predictions of specific behaviors, but is an attempt to describe an intrapsychic process over time—the activation of a particular impulse, the resulting anxiety, and the mobilization of a particular defense to combat the anxiety. Not only is such a formulation more difficult to verify independently, it is likely to be specific to the particular testing situation, as a different examiner or different circumstance might elicit different impulse-defense configurations.

Integration of Psychoanalytic and Empirical Approaches

Recently, there has been a growing interest in a rapprochement between the two camps. Can the two approaches to assessment be joined? What kinds of clinical questions are more appropriately addressed by which method, and how can data generated in one mode be interpreted in the other? In this section, I intend to address how a psychoanalytically-oriented clinician may approach the integration of empirical and analytic data, including a discussion of some caveats to this integration. In particular, I intend to present psychoanalytic object relations theory as an over-arching conceptual framework within which to analyze psychological test data.

One early approach to the integration of analytic and empirical approaches was to use different frames of reference for different sets of data. Nomothetic modes of analysis would be used for the analysis of structural data, while an analytic frame of reference would guide the interpretation of content. Erdberg (1993) noted, for example, that "theoretically-based" approaches to interpretation might best be integrated into a structural approach in the analysis of content (pp. 140). The problem with such an approach is that interpretations from two different conceptual frameworks are applied to different aspects of the data and combined without regard for the theoretical inconsistencies or contradictions that they may very well embody. It cannot make logical sense for one personality theory to apply to one set of data and for an entirely different theory to apply to another—especially when they are both used to describe to the same set of test results from the same patient. In such circumstances, the diagnosis and formulation often have little to do with one another, or worse, are mutually inconsistent. Personality assessment can only be conducted in the context of a coherent personality theory. Regardless of the approach taken to the data of assessment, a single theoretical framework is necessary if the resulting description is to be more than a collection of disconnected predictive statements of dubious validity. This point was made 40 years ago by Roy Schafer (1954) in his classic text *Psychoanalytic Interpretation in Rorschach Testing*, but often overlooked in recent years.

Weiner, in the Introduction to this volume, makes the important point that there is not—and cannot be—a single "Rorschach theory," because the Rorschach is a technique for data-gathering, not a psychology. In attempting to reconcile the analytic and empirical modes of analysis, he makes the useful distinction between the structure and the dynamics of personality. The former constitutes the enduring traits or dispositions of the individual that dictate his, characteristic modes of functioning, while the latter reflect the internal needs, conflicts, and defenses that are expressed in his relationships and his daily life. Empirical methods of Rorschach interpretation concentrate on describing the structure of personality, whereas analytic modes are most appropriate for elucidating dynamics. This differs from earlier approaches, in that the distinction Weiner makes is not between structure and content of the Rorschach protocol—i. e., between different classes of data—but between different areas of personality.

From a strictly psychoanalytic perspective, however, Weiner's approach is only a starting point. Terms such as "dispositions" or "traits," while useful descriptors when making predictions about behavior are not in themselves explanatory. They imply a "black box" psychology in which why an individual behaves in a particular way is irrelevant unless it leads directly to more accurate prediction. A psychoanalyst must ask the question: Why does this individual manifest this characteristic behavior pattern or these sets of traits? This question needs to be answered in terms of internal and/or interpersonal processes, i. e., in terms of dynamics. To do so requires a psychodynamic theory.

What framework—empirical or psychoanalytic—is most appropriate depends at least in part on the purposes for which the assessment is conducted. Clearly, in cases where testing is done as part of a research enterprise in which groups of subjects are compared, empirical methods must be applied. In the clinical arena, however, the situation is more complicated. When used for initial screening, for example, where little is known about the patient and determinations such as whether or not he or she would be a candidate for psychotherapy are to be made, a framework in which the interpretive statements are derived primarily empirically may suffice. In cases where the patient is well-known, and is being referred because of an impasse in treatment, or because of specific questions that the treating therapist has, such information may be insufficient. Piotrowski (1982)) argued that generally projective testers strove for statements that had a high degree of validity albeit low applicability, rather than statements of high applicability and lower validity. By this he meant statements that were highly specific to the particular subject of the testing although not easily generalizable, but that could be made with a very high degree of confidence. These statements are likely to be narrow in focus and were termed by Piotrowski, "microfacts." To know, for example, that a patient had a positive suicide constellation and was therefore a suicidal risk may be useful in an initial assessment, but is likely to be of limited value to the clinician who has been working with him or her and is already aware of this fact. Of greater utility would be the knowledge of under what circumstances and in what ways such an attempt is likely to occur or what are the unconscious conflicts and fantasies that are associated with the suicidality in order to know what to explore in psychotherapy. For this kind of information, the nomothetic approach has to be abandoned in favor of one that utilizes intra-individual comparisons. The tester is concerned not so much with how the patient's suicidality compares with that of other patients, but rather how it fits into the patient's psyche as a whole—what events are likely to stimulate a suicidal crisis, what are the conflicts that lead him to think of ending his life, what are the defenses he uses against these conflicts, and what causes these defenses to fail.

These two frameworks have been termed by others as reflecting the difference between testing and assessment, with the former being a process in which single traits or behavior patterns are isolated, measured, and predicted, while the second reflects primarily an integrative task in which the particular "fact" or datum is only considered in the context of the overall configuration of the individual's personality. Bolziger (1990) pointed out that this distinction actually reflected a fundamental split that has existed throughout the history of psychiatry. The strictly empirical approach actually harkens back to Rorschach himself and the Kraepelinian school in which the primary diagnostic task was to describe and categorize. Psychopathology was conceived of as a set of relatively static "syndromes." By contrast, the dynamic approach reflects an orientation that sees psychopathology in terms of a series of mental processes. Rather than diagnosing syndromes, the psychologist in this model sees as his or her task the elucidation of the underlying mental processes and how they inter-relate to create behavior pathology.

Given the different philosophical and theoretical meanings that derive from these different approaches, it should be clear that merely applying one model to one set of data and another to a different set of data about the same person cannot make heuristic sense. I will also submit that if one theoretical framework is to be used to incorporate both sets of data—quantative and dynamic—it must be the analytic one. This is not because of any inherent superiority of psychoanalytic theory. Rather, it is because the analytic framework, which conceives of personality in terms of observable phenomena and underlying dynamics is capable of explaining both levels of data, whereas a framework without a theory of underlying dynamics has no means of generating inferences at this level.

I propose that quantitative data be treated like any other observed phenomenon, subject to psychoanalytic interpretation. What this means is that the conventional empirically-derived interpretations of particular scores or configurations should not be seen as final statements, but as subject to further analysis. Rather than seeing extratensive or introversive as "types," they can be seen as observations about the patient's characteristic mode of handling affect. These in turn can be interpreted as reflecting a particular impulse-defense configuration, depending upon the dynamics of the particular case. What is lost in empirical rigor by extending the interpretation beyond the empirically verifiable is made up for by richness and applicability.

Before turning to a consideration of the object relations framework of assessment, I wish to make one other observation. Once one broadens one's interest from the strictly quantitative, certain changes in one's perception of the instrument itself follows. The Rorschach is traditionally considered a test of perception, a viewpoint explicit in the Comprehensive System, which is based upon a perceptual-cognitive model (Exner, 1986). From an analytic perspective, however, in which all data—whether quantitative or not—are taken into consideration, the test is not truly one of perception, so much as of communication. Strictly speaking, we do not analyze percepts, we analyze patient's communications about their perceptions. Indeed, we have no direct access to the patient's perceptions, only to his or her verbalizations. As a consequence, the nuances of language are often as important, if not more so, than the actual objects described. A patient may, for example, offer a percept of women, a popular response, to Card III of the Rorschach, but do so with language that clearly reflects his contempt or hostility toward them. If one merely considers the formal properties of the response, it may appear to be mundane, to communicate little information about the subject save his capacity to see popular human forms and his relatively intact reality testing. A consideration of the language used to describe this response to the examiner, however, reveals much about his inner world and his relationships to the objects in it. If we then add the relationship to the examiner into the equation—the same response told to a female examiner may reflect sadistic impulses toward women in authority, for example, whereas to a male examiner it may reflect a wish to ally with a powerful father in opposition to a devalued mother figure—the resulting interpretation becomes far richer and more complex, albeit more speculative.

Object Relations Theory as a Unifying Framework

The term "object relations theory" has gained considerable currency in recent years. Unfortunately, it is used rather loosely to refer to several different sets of ideas. In its narrowest meaning, it refers specifically to the psychoanalytic theory of personality developed by W. R. D. Fairbairn (1952). In a more common sense, it refers to the psychoanalytic theories from the so-called "British School," including the works of Melanie Klein, D. W. Winnicott, Michael Balint, etc., as well as Fairbairn. In its broadest meaning, it refers to any theory of personality that conceives of the personality primarily in terms of the subject's relationships, both internal and external. In this paper, I am using the term "object relations theory" in this broadest sense.

As I have argued elsewhere (Smith, 1991), object relations theory is uniquely suited for use in interpreting psychological test data. One particular advantage of the object relations framework is that its propositions are couched in relational terms which are more easily translated into inferences of direct utility to referring clinicians. Contrary to the assertions of Greenberg and Mitchell (1983), I do not hold that an object relations perspective is inconsistent with a theory that pays attention to the role of the drives. Rather an expanded object relations perspective pays considerable attention to such functions, but conceptualizes them as arising out of the mother-child interpersonal matrix. It is the relationship with the interpersonal environment that gives meaning to the instincts and form and structure to the ego. Psychopathology can be conceived of as a series of continua from less self-other differentiation to greater boundary clarity, from more primitive dependence to relative independence, and from dyadic to triadic relationships, rather than as a series of discrete disorders.

Of particular relevance is the work of Winnicott and his followers (Ogden, 1989; Winnicott, 1971). Winnicott proposed an intermediate stage between the omnipotent fantasy of earliest infancy in which external objects are experienced as a part of the self, and the acceptance of the existence of an external world independent of one's wishes. This stage is inhabited by the transitional object, an object which is simultaneously part of the external world and under the fantasied omnipotent control of the infant. In normal development, the infant gradually relinquishes the transitional object as he internalizes the capacity to soothe himself in the absence of the mother. It leaves in its wake, however, an intermediate zone of experience, called "potential space," in which the life-long task of reconciling internal and external reality can occur. For Winnicott, this is the location of symbolic thought, play, and cultural experience. Projective test responses, especially Rorschach percepts are transitional phenomena and occur in the potential space between reality and fantasy. They are, in Winnicott's words, simultaneously created and found. Created in the sense that the blot is an amorphous form that is given meaning by the subject's own perceptual and cognitive processes; found in that the resulting image must be reconciled with the attributes of the blot. In order to accomplish this task, the subject must form a relationship—albeit a transient one—with the object represented. It is this relationship that is of especial interest to the psychologist. Some subjects are unable to maintain the as if quality of the blot and thus form relationships with their percepts that are isomorphic with those they form with objects in their world. Others cannot seem to form any relationship, failing to enliven their percepts with any fantasy at all. They typically respond only to the form of the blot with highly constricted responses from which they distance themselves (insisting, for example, that the response was only given because the examiner insisted).

Further complicating this picture, of course, is the nature of the subject's relationship with the examiner—the testing transference-countertransferences. Not only are the subject's comments to and about the tester relevant data, but the actual responses are affected by this relationship. One may, for example, conceptualize a Rorschach testing as comprising three objects in triadic relationship. There is the examiner, the subject, and the blot itself. The subject's perceptions of each of these objects and the interrelationships among them can be complex and important. A competitive subject, for example may experience the examiner as a rival for the possession of the blot and feel the need to compete with him by producing more creative or clever responses than he (the examiner) could. At the same time, he may fear retribution from the examiner for his "oedipal victory." Another subject may shy away from letting his imagination go, for fear of penetrating the card, perceived as the exclusive domain of the examiner. While these dynamics are complex, difficult to ferret out, and often highly speculative, attention to them can only serve to enrich the process of test interpretation.

Analytic Interpretations of Empirical Data

Readers are undoubtedly familiar with the application of object relations theory to the clinical interpretation of verbalizations, sequence analysis, and subtle nuances of test behavior. Relatively less attention has been paid, however, to using this perspective in interpreting structural data. As mentioned above, the strategy I endorse is to consider the interpretations of structural data as data to be further analyzed and interpreted. Most of the interpretive statements generated from an empirical approach carry implicit assumptions of a trait psychology. Descriptive statements that are generated about the subject often describe him or her as a person of this or that kind. This kind of description can be greatly elaborated by further analysis. From an object relations perspective, we would seek to understand the particular trait in terms of the underlying conflicts, defenses, and self and object representations that produce it. Ideally, one would also like to be able to formulate a plausible developmental hypothesis for the observed patterns. In order to carry out this interpretive strategy, further evidence from a consideration of the nuances of language, content, and the relationship with the examiner are examined along with the structural data.

Let me give a brief clinical example. A 31 year old skilled laborer produced a protocol in which there were 9 positives on the Suicide Constellation, a positive Depression Index, and 9 Space responses. These findings were interpreted, in accordance with the Comprehensive System, as indicating an individual who was depressed, rageful, and acutely suicidal. Important as these findings are, they can be significantly refined if all of the data are taken into account and viewed from an object relations perspective. A careful look at the nature of the Space responses, for example, reveals a preoccupation with bodily interstices and a sense of hollowness. This coupled with the generally poor form of these responses as well as other observations (chiefly from the Structural Summary) that he lives in an object-less world, suggest that the preoccupation with white space may reflect more than mere anger or oppositionalism, but may constitute his attempts to represent his own sense of inner emptiness. Seen in this light, suicide, especially a murder-suicide, can be understood as an attempt to stave off a decompensation into an object-less void, a last-ditch effort to avoid a sense of nothingness by uniting in death with the valued—and hated—object. This interpretation suggests that it is specifically the threat of abandonment by someone in his world that is likely to precipitate suicidal or homicidal acting out. This fuller interpretation is likely to be of significance to a treating therapist who must not only attempt to anticipate future behavior, but try and understand the patient and his inner world as well.

The Paradox of Integration: Some Concluding Thoughts

In a recent paper, DeCato (1993) decried what he termed "monotheism" in Rorschach psychology, i. e., the tendency to insist that the test is a single instrument with one correct method of interpretation. In the past, this one correct method was psychoanalytic; today it is the Comprehensive System. A failure to recognize the potential contributions of different interpretive systems derived from different theoretical orientations is frequently a consequence of blind faith in a single approach. Differentiation and integration are the two primary aspects of psychological development. It is no different with the Rorschach.

Psychoanalytic and empirical approaches to the Rorschach are quite different and, as I have discussed, stem from different philosophical traditions. As such, there are serious pitfalls in any attempt to integrate them into a single approach to test data. A case in point is the discussion about the concept of "projection." Exner (1989), in a carefully-reasoned paper, argued that projection in the Rorschach could only be assumed to occur in those responses that deviated significantly from norms, or that were described in an over-elaborate or unusual manner. Most responses, he argued, were merely "best fit" answers. From an object relations viewpoint in which every response involves in some way the integration of internal representations with external perceptions, a more psychoanalytically-informed statement would be that projection is constant, but the nature of the projection can only be inferred when the response is unusual in one or another way.

This debate reflects different methods of approaching test data. In one, deviations from norms constitute the privileged data set, in the other, no *a priori* assumptions are made about what datum might reveal the most about the subject. The debate also reflects fundamentally different approaches to the basic question of Rorschach psychology: how does an individual's verbal responses to a set of inkblots come to reveal important aspects of his or her personality? This question, while interesting, is of little importance to a strict empiricist. It is sufficient that the responses predict behavior patterns as evidenced by lawful relationships between Rorschach variables and outcome measures. For a psychoanalyst, on the other hand, it is necessary to articulate the nature of the relationship between Rorschach responses and personality in order for interpretations of the patient's construction of meaning to make sense. For example, from the perspective of object relations theory, a preponderance of Human Detail responses suggests a lack of object constancy and a tendency to relate to others not as independent centers of initiative, but as part-objects who exist to satisfy or frustrate specific needs of the subject. From a Kleinian perspective, it might be further speculated that the subject relates primarily from the paranoid-schizoid position in which projective mechanisms of defense predominate. This kind of interpretation cannot be made solely from an empirically-derived relationship between Hd responses and some outcome measure such as a diagnosis of borderline personality disorder. Only a knowledge of the theory of object relations and a conceptualization of Human responses to the Rorschach as the projection of the internal object world into external reality as represented by the blot permits this kind of conceptualization. From a psychoanalytic perspective, the Rorschach is not a test, it is a method for eliciting data about the internal workings of the subject's psyche.

In this paper I have attempted to discuss how these two radically different approaches to testing might be brought together. I have argued that in order to integrate psychoanalytic and empirical methods, the analytic must provide the umbrella theoretical framework. How successfully this can ultimately be done is, to my mind, an open question. It may be that the underlying contradictions are so great that any attempt to integrate them into a single approach is doomed to failure. On the other hand, it is also possible that by considering the strengths of both methods, an approach to clinical assessment that is far more powerful may be forged. Regardless of the ultimate fate of current attempts at rapprochement, the effort can only serve to increase our knowledge of this infinitely complex method of personality assessment.

Résumé

Aujourd'hui, les perspectives dominantes en matière d'interprétation du Rorschach sont les méthodes psychanalytique et empirique, celleci tenant le haut du pavé aux Etats Unis, cellelà dans presque tout le reste du monde. Depuis quelque temps, on voit poindre un intérêt pour un éventuel rapprochement des deux approches. De quelle manière et dans quelle mesure une telle intégration pourrait se faire, cela constitue le sujet de cet article.

Il est montré que les traditions psychanalytique et empirique sont en fait le reflet de deux courants épistémologiques très différents appliqués au Rorschach. L'empirisme est issu du positivisme, dont le but est la prédiction d'événements (en l'occurrence le comportement d'un sujet) à partir de constatations. Les propositions sont vérifiables et réplicables. Au contraire, la psychanalyse est une science plus herméneutique, dont le but est non pas de prédire, mais de générer du sens. Les critères de pertinence d'une interprétation sont différents dans les deux approches, comme le sont les types d'interprétations formulées. En outre, différentes classes de données sont prises en compte. Par exemple, alors que l'approche empirique exige la réplicabilité, l'approche psychanalytique considère que beaucoup de données (généralement celles qui sont repérées à travers l'empathie), étant le produit d'une dyade spécifique examinateurexaminé, ne sont pas généralisables. Ce n'est pas qu'une approche serait meilleure que l'autre, car en fait, elles procurent des réponses différentes à des questions différentes.

Certaines tentatives antérieures d'intégration des deux approches sont ici critiquées dans la mesure où elles tendent à appliquer un type d'approche aux données structurales, et un autre à l'analyse des contenus. Elles débouchent sur des descriptions structurales et des formulations dynamiques souvent peu intégrables les unes aux autres. L'auteur soutient que, si l'on veut intégrer des modalités empirique et analytique, il faut disposer d'un cadre théorique unique qui les englobe. En outre, ce cadre ne pourra être que de nature analytique, car la théorie analytique est la seule à disposer d'un modèle pour comprendre la dynamique sousjacente.

Le cadre théorique le plus indiqué pour l'interprétation des données Rorschach semble donc être la théorie des relations d'objet. Ce modèle conçoit la personnalité et la psychopathologie en termes de relations aux objets, à la fois internes et externes. Dans cette perspective, l'auteur se réfère tout particulièrement aux travaux de Winnicott et de ses continuateurs, car la réponse Rorschach peut être assimilée à des phénomènes transitionnels qui prennent corps dans l'espace intermédiaire entre les mondes interne et externe.

Enfin, l'auteur suggère une stratégie pour l'interprétation analytique des données empiriques. Il propose de traiter les interprétations des données quantitatives comme des données en ellesmêmes, qui nécessitent de nouvelles analyse et interprétation. Ce processus exige un mouvement continuel d'allerretour entre les données structurales et les subtiles nuances des contenus, de l'expression verbale, et de la relation vivante examinateurexaminé. Cette stratégie est illustrée par un exemple.

L'article se termine par des remarques générales sur l'importance du pluralisme actuel dans la psychologie du Rorschach, et sur les perspectives d'intégration d'approches disparates.

Resumen

Los métodos psicoanalíticos y empíricos para la interpretación del Rorschach constituyen los paradigmas dominantes en la actualidad, imperando el segundo en los Estados Unidos y el primero en buena parte del reso del mundo. Ha habido recientemente un interés creciente en un posible acercamiento entre ambos enforques. Cómo y cuánto podría lograrse una integración es el tema de este trabajo.

Se argumenta que las tradiciones psicoanalítica y empírica reflejan en la actualidad la aplicación al Rorschach de dos epistemologías claramente diferentes. El empirismo se deriva del positivismo lógico, para el cual la meta es la predicción de eventos futuros (en este case una conducta del sujecto) a partir de observaciones. Las proposiciiones son refultables y replicables. En contraste, el psicoanálisis es una ciencia más hermenéutica en la cual el propósito no es la predicción sino la generación de significado. Los criterios para juzgar lo adecuado de una interpretación difieren de uno a otro enfozue, asi como el tipo de interpretaciones que se realizan. Además, pueden ser consideradas clases diferentes de datos. Por ejemplo, el enfoque empírico requiere replicabilidad, mientras que el psicoanalítico reconcoce que muchos datos (aquellos obtenidos a través de la empatía) constituyen el producto do la díada especifica examinador-examinado y no son, en consecuencia, generalizables. Ne es tanto que un enfoque sea mejor que el otro, sino más bien que proveen diferentes respuestas a diferentes preguntas.

Se critican los intentos previos de integración por su tendencia a aplicar en enfoque a los datos estructurales y otro al contenido. Ello conduce a descripciones estructuralies y formulaciones dinámicas que son frecuentemente contradictorias. Se arguye que si los modos empíricos y analíticos hand de ser integrados, debe haber un marco teórico único que los englobe. Incluso, si ambos tipos de datos, empíricos y dinámicos, son tomados en cuenta, deberá utilizarse el moarco analítico, debido a que sólo la teoria analítica tiende un modelo que dé cuenta de los dinamismos subyacentes.

Se propone en consequencia la teoría de las relaciones objectales como un marco teórico especialmente adequado para la interpretación de los datos del Rorschach. En este modelo, la personalidad y la psycopatología con concebidos en términos que las relaciones con objectos, tanto externos como internos. Se cita el trabajo de Winnicott Y sus seguidores como particularmente relevante para el Rorschach, ya que las respuestas al test pueden ser concebidas como fenómenos transicionales que se producen en un espacio intermedia entre los mundos externo e interno.

Finalmente, se ofrece una estratagia para la interpretación analítica de los datos empíricos de la prueba. Se sugiere que las interpretaciones de los datos cuantitativos sean también tratadas como datos, sujetos a su vez a análisis e interpretación. Ello requiere un movimiento fluido, de uno a otro, entre los datos estructurales y los matices sutiles del contenido, la expresión verbal y la relación en curso entre el examinador y el examinado. Se dá un ejemplo de esta estrategia.

Esta contribución concluye con algunos comentarios generales acerce de la importancia del pluralismo en la psicología del Rorschach en la actualidad, y acerce de los perspectivas de integradión de enfoques dispares.

References

Arnow, D., & Cooper, S. (1988). Toward a Rorschach psychology of the self. In H. Lerner & P. Lerner (Eds.), *Primitive mental states and the Rorschach* (pp. 53–70). New York: International Universities Press.

Blatt, S., & Lerner, H. (1982). Investigations in the Psychoanalytic Theory of Object Relations and Object Representations. In J. Masling (Eds.), *Empirical Studies on Psychoanalytic Theories* (pp. 159–188). Hillsdale, NJ: The Analytic Press.

Bolziger, A. (1990). Hiatus methodologique entre le Rorschach et la clinique inconvenients et remedes. *Rorschachiana, 17*, 66–72.

Cooper, S., & Arnow, D. (1986). An object relations view of the borderline defenses: A review. In M. Kissen (Eds.), *Assessing Object Relations Phenomena* (pp. 143–171). New York: International Universities Press.

DeCato, C. (1993). On the Rorschach M response and monotheism. *Journal of Personality Assessment, 60*(2), 362–378.

Erdberg, P. (1993). The U. S. Rorschach scene: Integration and elaboration. In I. B. Weiner (Eds.), *Rorschachiana: Yearbook of the International Rorschach Society* (pp. 139–151). Bern, Switzerland: Hogrefe & Huber.

Exner, J. (1989). Searching for Projection in the Rorschach. *Journal of Personallity Assessment, 53*, 520–536.

Exner, J. E. (1986). *The Rorschach: A Comprehensive System. Volume 1: Basic Foundations* (2nd. ed.). New York: Wiley.

Fairbairn, W. (1952) *Psychoanalytic studies of the personality*. London: Routledge & Kegan Paul.

Greenberg, S., & Mitchell, S. (1983). *Object Relations in Psychoanalytic Theory*. Cambridge, MA: Harvard University Press.

Kissen, M. (Ed.). (1986). *Assessing Object Relations Phenomena*. Madison, CT: International Universities Press.

Kohut, H. (1971). *The analysis of the self*. New York: International Universities Press.

Kwawer, J., Lerner, H., Lerner, P., & Sugarman, A. (Ed.). (1980). *Borderline Phenomena and the Rorschach*. New York: International Universities Press.

Lerner, H., & Lerner, P. (Ed.). (1988). *Primitive Mental States and the Rorschach*. Madison, CT: International Universities Press.

Lerner, P. (1991). *Psychoanalytic Theory and the Rorschach*. Hillsdale, NJ: Analytic Press.

Mayman, M. (1967). Object representations and object relationships in Rorschach responses. *Journal of Projective Techniques and Personality Assessment, 31*, 17–24.

Ogden, T. (1989). Playing, dreaming, and interpreting experience: comments on potential space. In M. Fromm & B. Smith (Eds.), *The facilitating environment: Clinical applications of Winnicott's theory.* (pp. 255–278). Madison, CT: International Universities Press.

Piotrowski, Z. (1982). Unsuspected and unintended microfacts in personology. *American Psychologist, 37,* 190–196.

Rapaport, D. (1952). Projective Techniques and the Theory of Thinking. *Journal of Projective Techniques, 16,* 269–275.

Rapaport, D., Gill, M., & Schafer, R. (1968). *Diagnostic Psychological Testing* (Revised edition). New York: International Universties Press.

Ricoeur, P. (1970). *Freud and Philosophy: An Essay in Interpretation.* New Haven, CT: Yale University Press.

Schafer, R. (1948). *The Clinical Application of Psychological Tests.* New York: International Universities Press.

Schafer, R. (1954). *Psychoanalytic Interpretation in Rorschach Testing.* New York: Grune & Stratton.

Schwartz, F., & Lazar, Z. (1979). The Scientific Status of the Rorschach. *Journal of Personality Assessment, 43,* 3–11.

Smith, B. (1990). The origins of interpretation in the countertransference. *Psychoanalytic Psychology, 7* (suppl.): 89–104.

Smith, B. (1991). Theoretical Matrix of Interpretation. *Rorschachiana, 17,* 73–77.

Stolorow, R., Brandchaft, B., & Atwood, G. (1987). *Psychoanalytic treatment: An intersubjective approach.* Hillsdale, NJ: The Analytic Press.

Winnicott, D. (1971). *Playing and Reality.* London: Tavistock Books.

Projective Approach to Personality Study in Soviet Psychology: A Summary of Research

Leonid F. Burlatchuk

Kiev University, Kiev, Ukraine

Elena Yu. Korzhova

Professional Training Research Institute, St. Petersburg, Russia

At the end of 1991 the USSR dissolved and Soviet psychological science ceased to exist. The majority of psychologists presumably have not yet perceived that present-day investigations constitute the foundation of national psychological schools that will still have to find their place in the world of psychological science.

This article is devoted to the development of projective approaches to the study of personality in Soviet psychology and summarizes certain directions such studies have taken. Our main purpose is to acquaint professionals with the work of Soviet scientists that is not well known abroad.

Studies With the Rorschach Test
Before the Projective Period

The Rorschach Test began attracting attention in this country shortly after it was published by its author in 1921. One of the first significant studies with the Rorschach Test was reported by Petrova (1927). In this study the author distinguished types of "endogenous" responses in connection with two types of psychological constitution, namely, affective-abstractive and concrete-emotional types.

At about the same time, innovative studies with the Rorschach test were carried out at the Kiev Psychoneurological Institute, the Ukrainian

78

Psychoneurological Institute, and the All-Ukrainian Institute of Hygiene in Education, which existed in the 1920s-1930s. This work confirmed for the first time after Rorschach the data he had obtained in studying patients with epilepsy (Hakkebush et al., 1928). The first work on the diagnosis of psychopathology (Phundiler & Smirnova, 1928) and the exposition of latent pathological complexes (Matskevich, 1930) with the Rorschach Test were also discussed at this early time. It is quite clear, however, that these investigations of the 1920s and 1930s did not utilize a projective approach, which would be formulated later.

A tendency to take an ideological view of such psychological studies became clearly manifest in the 1930s. There was a wave of criticism of tests as instruments of personality study that entailed in fact prohibition of scientific research in psychological diagnostics. The tests were considered to be not only useless, but also harmful. Our history had shown that personality could be assessed by other criteria, such as social class membership, personal devotion to the leader, and the like. In national psychology for a long time notions about hazards of endorsing tests and about the damage they could cause were clung to firmly. The Party Central Committee adopted a decree in 1936 that banned these so-called "senseless" tests. Soviet psychology suffered greatly from its struggles with being cast as "ideological perversions" and "bourgeois conceptions"; its development was thereby isolated from the development of world science for a long time.

Studies in the 1960s and 1970s

The process of rehabilitating tests and psychodiagnostic studies began in the 1960s and was directly connected with well-known changes in the political climate of the country. First of all, tests began to be applied in clinical psychology, which was relatively neutral with respect to ideology. Only a very small circle of professionals conversant with foreign publications knew about projective techniques at this time. Nevertheless, these methods, first of all the Rorschach, started to become used in clinical diagnostic evaluations. In addition, the first studies began to appear showing that projective techniques not only competed favorably with well-known traditional techniques, but surpassed them in the depth and comprehensiveness with which they could assess personality functioning.

79

It is useful to cite several typical studies from that era. The problem of diagnosing psychotic delirium among presenile patients was studied by Mendelevich (1966). Using the Rorschach, Vein and Vlasova (1966) examined emotionality in patients with focal disorders of the limbic-reticular system; Stanishevskaya and Huldan (1972) introduced forensic examination. Initial steps were taken to familiarize psychologists with the TAT (Gilyasheva, 1964, 1967), the Incomplete Sentences (Rumyantsev, 1969), and the Picture Frustration (PF) Study (Tarabrina et al., 1971). At that time one of the authors of the present article had begun to study the patients with schizophrenia and epilepsy with the Rorschach Test (Burlatchuk, 1971, 1972, 1974).

The experimental studies of that period were characterized by (a) efforts to demonstrate the diagnostic value of projective techniques, which was not being acknowledged in clinical research, and (b) efforts to define the place and importance of projective techniques in revealing individual personality features among patients with psychological disorders. This was a time when projective techniques were being rediscovered, and, as a result, the studies of the period tended to be somewhat fragmentary. The fragmentary nature of this research was particularly evident with respect to the most complicated of projective techniques, the Rorschach Test, on which the work clearly reflected the lack of scientific traditions and literature.

Very commonly during this time, research reports were limited merely to stating the differences obtained for various indices in comparing clinical groups. Researchers avoided interpretations of the data obtained (or interpreted them very prudently), because they did not want to risk coming into conflict with officially accepted theories in Soviet psychology and psychiatry. Moreover, projective methods were widely viewed as psychoanalytic techniques, and psychoanalysis was not regarded as a scientific theory in the USSR. This view and the belief that projective techniques were directed toward the study of unconscious personality processes contributed substantially to avoidance of interpreting the data obtained with projective methods. In this regard, it is important to note that Soviet psychologists borrowed from foreign literature the assumption that the psychoanalytic concept of projection accounts for the nature of the response process in projective techniques.

Further development of research with projective techniques was being severely restricted at this time by lack of analysis of the theoretical conceptions on which they were based. We must emphasize that the postulated direct connection of projective techniques with psychoanalytic theory was leading in this country to their exclusion from scientific endeavors in personality research. Fortunately, however, important articles of that period concerning the concept of projection and different ways of formulating the theoretical basis of projective techniques in personality research helped greatly to overcome the incorrect notion that projective techniques depended on psychoanalytic theory (Myasishchev et al., 1969; Savenko, 1971; Burlatchuk, 1972, 1979). For example, the mechanisms underlying projective techniques were proposed by Norakidze (1975) to involve concepts of context, by Sokolova (1979) to involve attribution of personality meaning, and by Burlatchuk (1979) to be based on perception as an aspect of personality functioning.

The monograph *Personality Study in Clinical Psychology On the Basis of the Rorschach Test* (Burlatchuk, 1979) summarized the research of the 1960s–1970s in projective psychology in general and regarding clinical applications of the Rorschach in particular. This was the first monograph published in the country that was devoted to projective techniques in the study of personality. The monograph described foreign and Soviet conceptions of the theoretical basis of the projective approach and the technique of applying the Rorschach Test; presented implications of the results of clinical studies; reported data obtained in patients with schizophrenia and epilepsy; and, finally, focused attention on the need to develop studies in this area and the relevance of such work to perspectives on the nature of cognition.

Studies of the 1980s and Early 1990s

Methodological and theoretical research with projective techniques continued during the 1980s and into the 1990s. Modern foreign conceptions of projective techniques, issues concerning the theoretical basis of the projective approach, and the role of studies with projectives in understanding unconscious processes were analyzed by Burlatchuk (1989 a, 1989 b). The author placed primary emphasis on the notion that perceptual activity and the personal nature of perceptual processes provide the basic foundation for explaining and analyzing projective phenomena. Projective techniques were conceived by Burlatchuk as methods of personality investigation based on the construction by the subjects of specific ambiguous stimulus situations that create favorable

81

conditions for the manifestation of tendencies, attitudes, emotional states, and other personality features through perceptual activity.

The nature of the projective approach was formulated further as a means of cognition in developing the concept of "measured individuality" in psychodiagnosis. As a mid-range theory, this formulation is intermediate between global theoretical formulations, and the theory accordingly fills a gap in the system of results of psychological knowledge (Burlatchuk & Korzhova, 1993).

A study by Sokolova (1980) constituted both a theoretical and methodological investigation and also a training guideline for application. Following the activity theory, it was suggested that projective data should be interpreted on the basis of categories of personal meaning. Specific personality characteristics identified with projective techniques can then be described in terms of personal meanings and appropriate activities in which a person finds or attempts to deny personal meanings. This approach is applicable to methods of interpretation, as in the TAT. Because the projective situation creates opportunities for displays of action tendencies, the examiner needs to learn from the data obtained the personal meaning to the subject of particular motives and the circumstances likely to provoke actions. From Sokolova'a point of view, the projective approach is intended first of all to identify conflictual thoughts and feelings. This perspective narrowed the range of personality manifestations that could be understood through the projective approach.

Etkind (1981) analyzed theoretical issues concerning projective techniques and conceptualized connections between perception and personality in terms of an isomorphism between two structures—the sensory substance of perceptual images on one hand and an affect-cognition unity in personality on the other. The history of projective approaches to personality diagnosis in our country and abroad was also a subject of analysis by Sokolova (1987).

Contemporary experience with projective methods in other countries has also been a subject of study. One analysis of contemporary work was presented at the International Congress of Rorschach and Other Projective Methods in 1990 (Burlatchuk & Korzhova, 1991).

Work With Well-Known Methods

Recent research efforts have also involved working with well-known methods to develop new indices, improve their standardization, and modify them in ways that would expand their diagnostic utility.

Developing New Indices in Well-Known Methods

Among new developments in older techniques, Uriev (1982) suggested a method of quantitative evaluation of deviations from normative expectation in studies with the Luscher Color Test. A new system of interpreting data obtained with the Szondi test was worked out, in which a computer-generated analysis suggests a statistically valid transformation of the results of a 5-item rating of the Szondi cards into four of Cattell's secondary factors: extraversion, anxiety, rationalism, and independence (Dobrovich, 1990).

Standardizing Well-Known Methods

Tarabrina (1984) standardized the PF-Study and published a handbook devoted to this method. The Luscher Color Test was validated by Petrenko and Kucherenko (1988), who specified symbolic meanings of colors, preferences for which were provoked in different emotional states with special methods of suggested called "Psychosynthesis." The data they obtained provided a fresh perspective on the issue of color symbolism, particularly with respect to relationships between associations to color and personal experiences of the individual.

Stepanova (1989) studied the validity of the Free Self-Description Method. The obtained data made it possible to represent products of creativity in the form of an unstructured test, and this feature of the method identifies its similarity to projective techniques.

Presently, elaborations of method are underway in the field of psychogeometry, and a handbook concerning *Psychogeometry for Managers* has recently been published (Alexeev & Gromova, 1991). Studies on the standardization of their method are being carried out. Homentauskas (1985) has suggested a variation of the Family Drawing Technique involving a complex and differentiated scoring system. His approach analyzes the structure of the test, specific aspects of the graphic presentation of family members, and specific aspects of the process of drawing.

Modifying Well-Known Methods

Hersonsky (1988) suggested that the pictogram should be considered a projective technique. By modifying the procedures for administering the measure and the system for interpreting the scores, he was able to extract information about the personality of subjects being tested. In other work the stimulus material of the Szondi test was used as a basis for developing the Social-Perceptual Intuitive Test (Kuznetsov et al., 1986). This test was created to define difficulties in interpersonal relationships in the area of social perception and to examine specific value orientations. The PF-Study was used as a basis for designing the Business Situations Test, which has been standardized and used as a means of investigating personality characteristics of engineers (Hitrova, 1992). A modification of the Incomplete Sentences was suggested by Kazachkova (1988, 1989) to provide specific definitions of affective and cognitive components of attitudes toward a wide range of people and situations. Kazachkova reported being able with this method to create an emotional profile of personality and define individual features of social intellect.

Expanding Diagnostic Utility of Well-Known Methods

The diagnostic utility of the PF-Study has been investigated through construct validation with other projective techniques, in particular the R. Gille Test-Film (Lubovsky, 1990). Diagnostic applications of the Rorschach Test were examined by Bely (1985) in a developmental study of visual perception in children and an analysis of visual perception in patients with unilateral brain tumors. It was suggested that good responses in the Rorschach Test require both maturity of brain structures and healthy functioning of these structures. It was suggested further that a high $F+\%$ may indicate the well-being of certain brain structures located in the right hemisphere, whereas S responses may indicate the activity and plasticity of perception provided by left hemisphere structures.

Bely's research has typically focused on basic perceptual functioning and its emotional and physiological substrates, without attention to personality variables. Research studies by Bespalko have been somewhat more concerned with the level of personality functioning in psycho-pathology; thus movement responses (*M*) are seen as reflecting the level of inner-directedness that serves as a basis of internal self-regulation, and *FM* responses are seen as reflecting the absence of self-regulation in depression (Bespalko & Gilyasheva, 1983). *Cn* (color naming) responses are seen as a primitive reaction to color that is associated with right-hemisphere pathology. Bespalko developed a catalogue of *D* responses and popular responses (*P*), including 108 distinctive *D* locations. *P* responses are considered by Bespalko to be the most informative index in discriminating between normal and pathological subjects. He has created special diagnostic tables listing the most characteristic responses found among persons with different mental disorders.

In other work, Sokolova (1985, 1989) reported positive results in applying the Family Rorschach in family counseling as an expressive method of diagnosing disturbances in family relationships. Yanshin (1989) conducted theoretical and empirical studies substantiating the utility of projective drawings. Data obtained with the Non-Existent Animals Drawing Test were compared with findings from the semantic differential technique and the PF-Study. Projective drawings were taken as graphic statements by the person being assessed as to his or her inner world and personality traits, using hypothesized parallels between verbal-metaphorical and image-graphical lines as the basis of interpretation. The hypothesis was proved through comparisons of the semantics of space in the drawings with linguistic cultural archetypes of metaphorical space.

In a study by Gabidulina (1986) with this test it was proposed that fantasy images would reflect the self-image of subjects being examined in the context of an unstructured relationship between subject and examiner in an atmosphere of frank collaboration. Baram (1986) examined the possibility of graphological diagnosis of neuroticism in states of tension by taking into account variability in the movement of the hand during the writing process.

New Projective Techniques

New projective techniques have also been developed in recent times. Bazhin and Etkind (1985) formulated the Color Attitudes Test, which was designed to study emotional components of subjects' attitudes toward significant other persons in their lives and to reflect both conscious and partly unconscious levels of these attitudes. The technical basis of the test is a color-association experiment using the set of color-stimuli from the Luscher Color Test, and confirmation of the validity of this test was reported.

A method of color evaluation of emotional states was suggested by Nikitina and Urvantsev (1988) for studying the structure and dynamics of affective experience in patients with neuroses. This test was validated through comparisons of differing patient groups, and the data also indicated that impressions and preferences among colors could help to specify the prognosis of the subjects' disorder.

Stolin (1982) suggested the Method of Projection Management Test for diagnosing the nature of self-perceptions. The examination procedures call for subjects to present their own verbal self-portrait on various diagnostic methods as it would be seen by another person and also as perceived by the subject. The distinctive features of self-attitudes and self-perception of personality traits, as differing from perceptions attributed to others, were examined. The findings validated the method, and meaningful qualitative analysis or content analysis of the data obtained was possible. Vizgina and Stolin (1989) have also used this method to study inner activities of personality.

As a further innovation, the "Sinta" method was developed by Alehina (1990) to obtain information about the subjective experience of emotional tension on the basis of analyzing the verbal content of statements. Sinta is thus a verbal projective technique and may be applied in evaluating personality dynamics in affect-arousing situations.

Also created was the Verbal Projective Test (Bleikher, Bokov, & Tashlikov, 1991). The stimulus material of this test consists of one two series of cards, a primary serious and a second series for parallel testing. The person being examined must make up a 5-minute story consisting of one sentence for each card. The story must indicate the present context of each sentence, its past origins, and its future outcome. The sentences given tend to be short, unstructured, broad in topic, and highly emotionally saturated. The data obtained may be interpreted in a traditional personal-pathopsychological manner (as with methods like the TAT) and in a lexical-grammatical fashion. This method has been applied in clinical psychological studies of neurotic patients and of schizophrenic patients with neurotic-like symptoms.

Faizullaev (1990) suggested another new method for studying projective attributions, a method for investigating self-regulatory motivations in personality functioning. With this method one can define attributive positions or approaches. Another method called Indirect Measurement of the Self-Evaluation System (IMSS) was worked out by Phedotova (1985) as a synthesis of projective and semantic approaches to personality diagnosis. Schematic portrayals of human faces are used as the stimulus material, and an adequate level of validity and reliability has been reported.

Babina and Shmelev (1982) created the Test of Humorous Phrases, which is a projective technique for diagnosing motivational aspects of personality functioning. This test, now standardized, consists of 80 humorous phrases, 40 of which are related to just one of 10 themes, and the other 40 of which are polythematic. Subjects taking the test are asked to classify the cards with humorous phrases. Finally among new methods, Yevdokimov (1986, 1987) developed and standardized the Projective Aviation Test (PAT) for evaluation of professionally important personality characteristics in students of aviator schools.

As pointed out earlier, the main orientation of research in projective psychology continues to be toward clinical psychology. Especially noteworthy have been investigations of personality characteristics in patients with neuroses. Bertok (1987) studied manifestations of life style of hysterical patients using the TAT and Incomplete Sentences. The possibility of making an initial diagnosis of neurotic functioning was investigated by Mitskene (1990) with the Luscher Color Test.

Psychological mechanisms of the etiology of neurosis were examined with a modified PF-Study by Mendelevich (1990); the data were used in particular to study the psychological impact of context on adequate reaction patterns. The Color Attitudes Test was used by Sermyagina and Etkind (1991) to explore ways in which family dynamics induce neurotic states.

Eidemiller and Cheremisin (1990) created a diagnostic combination of the Buss-Darke Inquiry and the Hand Test for studying the mechanisms of borderline and somatic disorders in adolescents. In the view of the present author, this kind of test combination opens up new vistas in the study of aggressiveness. Sobchik (1990) described the results of comparing the Luscher Color Test with data obtained using the Szondi, MMPI, TAT, and Rorschach in examinations of neurotic patients.

Projective techniques have been used often in studies of psychosomatic patients. Defense mechanisms in patients treated with hemodialysis were investigated using Incomplete Sentences, the Luscher Color Test, and the PF-Study by Lebedev, Petrova, and Vasilyeva (1991). Nicolayeva (1987) reported TAT data obtained from patients suffering from liver diseases; this work identified a reduction of time perspective, with restriction to the present moment. Gubachev, Ananyev, and Simanenkov (1988) in a personal-typological approach to studying patients with peptic ulcer, used the PF-Study, the Heckhausen Apperceptive Test, the Color Attitudes Test, and the Luscher Color Test, as well as neurohormonal methods. Three types of personality in patients with peptic ulcer were identified: passive-heteronomous, active-autonomous, and steady.

Aivasyan, Zaitsev, and Taravkova (1989) studied patients with cardiac disease, including hypertension and cardiac arrythmia. They found that the distribution of such patients according to the color position chosen differed from usual indices in healthy and unhealthy patients. The particular psychological characteristics of patients with cardiac diseases based on their color preferences were studied, an index of psychological adaptation on the Luscher Color Test was developed. This index made it possible to assess the anxiety level, the level of social adaptation. and the intrapsychic dynamics of cardiac patients.

In a study of psychological characteristics of patients with hypertensive disease by Aivasyan and Taravkova (1990), a brief version of the Luscher Color Test was used and the validity of the test was examined. Basilevich, Kukes, Alperovich et al. (1991) studied the relationship between coronary disease and personality characteristics with the Indirect Measure of Self-Evaluation System. In further studies of distinctive personality features in patients with acquired heart disease, methods were developed for identifying specific features of an individual's psychological time (Korzhova, 1991; Burlatchuk & Korzhova, 1992). It was suggested in these studies that personality changes influenced by disease and social circumstances were reflected in the specific details of psychological time.

Personal and situational dimensions of cardiac patients were specified using when the repertory grid Role Positions-Personal Traits and Psychological Autobiography methods. The development of these methods involved combination of semantic and life-span approaches. The methods were directed at the model of "subjective reality," that is, at comparing diagnostic results to the specificity with which individual protocols reflect fragments of objective reality. All of these techniques were characterized by a heavy reliance on projected material. Typically, psychologically similar groups of patients with acquired heart disease were identified and classified according to different forms of person-situation interaction.

Psychological characteristics specific to patients with schizophrenia were also studied with projective techniques. Bely (1991) applied the Rorschach method to the study of patients with delusional forms of schizophrenia. Patients with acute affective delusional syndromes saw in the blots unusual details and gave pathological responses reflecting affective tension and disorders of perception and thinking. In patients with systematized delusions, the subjects' interpretations of the blots were similar to those of normal subjects.

Specific Rorschach and TAT characteristics of patients with paraphrenic syndromes was studied by Rogovin and Polivyanaya (1988), whose intention was to differentiate chronic schizophrenia from schizoid personality. Lapin (1990) studied reactions to placebo among patients with schizoaffective disorders using the Luscher Color Test. Those patients who were nonreactive to placebo were characterized by stable choices in each of four samples; that is, after taking placebo these negative reactors did not change the initial stability or instability of their choices on the test.

Dragunskaya (1984) applied the Rorschach as the principal technique in studying emotional and cognitive processes in patients with endogenous depression. Data obtained in the psychodiagnostic study of depressed patients were compared to data obtained in phases of remission. The results demonstrated the role of all of the psychological processes studied in determining the qualitative nature of these patients' depression. The measured stability of emotional processes was directly proportional to the clarity and constriction of the cognitive processes observed and inversely proportional to the level of cognitive generalization.

These results may provide additional criteria to facilitate precise diagnosis of depression. Dragunskaya (1990) suggested further the quantification of Rorschach color responses in order to examine correlations between the elementary parameters of emotional and cognitive processes in endogenous depressions. The obtained correlations indicated some connection between general psychological aspects of relatedness and emotional and cognitive processes.

Belaya (1981) studied interparoxysmal characteristics of patients with epilepsy localized primarily in the left or right cerebral hemisphere. Using the Rorschach, new data were obtained concerning differing features of visual attention, perception, thinking, emotionality, and motor behavior in patients with epilepsy depending on the laterality of their brain lesion. Two variants of a "Rorschach epileptical syndrome" ("right-hemisphered" and "left-hemisphered") were described.

Perception of Rorschach forms was examined in patients with tumors of the frontal lobes by Bely (1980). Statistically significant differences were found in the interpretation of the figures depending on the affective influence. Comparison of the data obtained with historical data suggested that the differences in perception of forms among patients with brain lesions were determined to a greater degree by the lateralization of the pathological process than by the etiology of the disease.

Projective techniques were also applied in the practice of psychotherapy. The PF-Study was used in research on the psychotherapy of stuttering by Rau (1984). Gromov and Yakunina (1987) used the PF-Study and Incomplete Sentences in studying the rehabilitation process of patients with epilepsy. In situations of frustration, these patients were disposed to extrapunitive reactions in ego-defensive situations and extrapunitive forms of behavior in dealing with interpersonal conflicts. Voskresensky (1991) examined psychological influences on differences in the effects of suggestion by comparing TAT data obtained before hypnosis and following hypnotic suggestion of different interpretations of the TAT pictures. The findings contributed to understanding the mechanisms of unsuccessful psychotherapeutic interventions when patients were in a deep trance state.

A survey of the use of projective techniques in clinical settings by Bespalko and Gilyasheva (1983) revealed that the most widely used psychodiagnostic methods were the TAT, the PF-Study, Incomplete Sentences, the semantic differential technique (which has some features in common with projective methods), and the Rorschach.

Certain notions concerning the place of projective techniques in clinical psychodiagnosis were formed during these years of active research. The main value of these methods was felt to lie in their potential for yielding data about idiographic manifestations of "disease stereotypes" and providing clarity concerning the degree of psychological impairment in each individual case. On the other hand, individual diagnosis based on projective techniques may result in flagrant errors. To arrive at an accurate diagnostic conclusion, it is necessary to compare test results in the individual case with the generally known clinical characteristics of a disorder and not to operate blind with respect to well-known formulations for interpreting the data. It is necessary also to take adequate account of the individual's life history.

As a further distinctive feature of psychodiagnostic research, most authors have tended to consider not only the nosologic diagnosis of patients, as investigated with projective techniques, but also their main presenting symptoms and the course of their disorder. Working in this way, these researchers have avoided the narrow-mindedness of investigators who devote themselves solely to searching for psychodiagnostic indices of "schizophrenia in general" or of "characterological disorder" as a diagnostic entity.

Projective techniques in child and educational psychology have been used mainly with adolescents, especially those identified as "maladjusted" or "difficult." Matveev and Lebedev (1984) studied relationships between the attitudes of maladjusted adolescents and their personality traits using the Szondi Test. The results established some relationships between particular attitudes and personality traits and the types of maladaptive reactions being manifest. In a study of personality in adolescents with deviant behavior, the Incomplete Sentences and Family Drawing Technique were applied by Zaika, Dreidun, and Yachina (1990) to assess attitudes toward the future and social relationships.

Ustimenko (1984) studied the interpersonal relationships of "difficult" adolescents who had been running away from home with the Gila Test. The majority of these adolescent runaways showed little affection for their parents and other family members and held negative attitudes toward their teachers, but showed strong ties to their peers.

In work with adolescents belonging to nihilistic groups with nontraditional life styles, compared to adolescents not affiliated with such groups and psychologically disturbed adolescents, data from the Non-Existent Animals Drawing Test revealed unconventional images, alienation, interpersonal discomfort, demonstrativeness, reserve, aggressiveness, anxiety, and infantilism to an extent comparable with personality traits associated with the concept of "schizoidia" (Ivanova, Honcharov, & Papavasiliu, 1989).

Self-evaluation of juvenile delinquents with the Indirect Measure of Self-Evaluation was studied by Balitskas and Hippenreiter (1989). Associations were found between unfavorable conditions of development and upbringing in the family and at school and formation in children of a low self-evaluation. The data suggest that, if numerous attempts to raise self-evaluation by socially acceptable methods do not bring desirable results, a child may turn to antisocial patterns of behavior and to asocial values, following which the level of his or her self-evaluation may be observed to rise.

Other researchers have studied children reared in boarding schools, using the method of identifying corrections in personality (Mukhina, 1989); features of pathologic personality development in deaf children with the Luscher Color Test and the Non-Existent Animals Drawing (Sarayev & Kozlov, 1991); and aspects of motivation in adolescents with habit disorders (Tolstih & Kulakov, 1989). Older students have been studied with the TAT (Bibrih & Vasilyev, 1987) and with the Rorschach Test and the Luscher Color Test (Zakharova, 1991), and the professional self-consciousness of teachers has been examined with the PF-Study (Mitina, 1990).

Projective techniques have also been employed in the psychology of work, vocational counseling, and personnel selection. Psychological traits of drivers were examined in connection with their manner of steering using the PF-Study (Polyanova, 1988). Professional fitness of students in aviator schools was studied with the TAT, the Rorschach Test, and the PF-Study (Tugushev, 1982). Makhunina (1992) studied different professional groups and secondary school graduates with the Luscher Color Test to identify their professional interests. Lvonikov, Ponomarenko, and Tsuvarev (1988) applied the Luscher Color Test and the PF-Study to create a system for professional psychological selection of aviators and researchers.

Projective technique have been applied in social psychology as adjunct methods in studying the psychodiagnostic status of supervisors with the Luscher Color Test (Sobchik & Oobanova, 1989: the attitudes of executives toward supervisors with the TAT (Hittelmakher, 1991); future perspectives regarding nuclear threat with the pictogram (Roshchin & Kabachenko, 1987); and the nature of marital relationships with the PF-Study, the Szondi Test, and the Luscher Color Test (Volkova & Trapeznikova, 1985).

In the psychology of sports and the psychology of extreme conditions individual and typical reactions have been studied in extrapunitive and intropunitive sportsmen with the PF-Study and the Myokinetic Method (Romanina, 1990). Also studied have been the behavior of people in conditions of prolonged sleep deprivation (Zarakovsky & Stupnitsky, 1987) and, with the TAT, psychological state under the influence of unfavorable factors (Makhnatch, 1991).

Epilogue

Research on projective techniques occupied a peripheral place in Soviet psychology and was considered of minor importance. Very often progress in research was artificially restrained for ideological reasons. As a result there was a definite gap between theory and practice and between the level of research at home and abroad. What studies there were in this area were carried out by a small group of enthusiasts without any official support. Nevertheless, projective techniques gradually found their way into the applied work of practicing psychologists, due to the efforts of these enthusiasts. Projective techniques have now become an integral aspect of psychological practice. Only time will tell how fruitfully scientists will be able to purse projective studies of personality, and escape the legacy of Soviet psychology in this regard, in the independent countries that have arisen in the territory of the former USSR.

Acknowledgments

The authors would sincerely like to thank with pleasure the President of the International Society of Rorschach and Other Projective Methods, Prof. Nina Rausch de Traubenberg, and Dr. Irving B. Weiner, whose invitation and support contributed so much to the appearance of this article.

Résumé

Cet article retrace le développement de la recherche en matière de techniques projectives dans la psychologie soviétique et résume les études projectives de la personnalité. On décrit d'abord les premiers travaux Rorschach dans les années 20 et 30, avant la période des études projectives. Vers 1930, les tests furent interdits en tant qu'instruments d'étude de la personnalité car ils étaient considérés comme des "perversions idéologiques" issues de "conceptions bourgeoises." C'est ainsi que la psychologie soviétique fut pour de longues années isolée des développements qu'elle connut dans le reste du monde scientifique.

C'est dans les années 60 que l'on commença à réhabiliter les tests et les études psychodiagnostiques, en raison d'un changement survenu dans le climat politique du pays. On démontra alors l'utilité diagnostique des techniques projectives en recherche clinique et on montra qu'ils contribuaient de façon pertinente à identifier des caractéristiques de personnalité des patients psychologiquement perturbés. La recherche clinique consistait alors surtout à trouver des indices qui permettraient de différencier des groupes de patients en fonction de leurs réponses au test. On menait aussi des recherches théoriques portant sur les concepts de projection importés d'autres pays, et visant à investiguer des approches novatrices.

Dans les années 1980–1990 on vit fleurir des études méthodologiques et théoriques. La recherche s'est alors attachée à développer de nouveaux indices dans les méthodes connues, à améliorer leur standardisation, et à les modifier pour accroître leur efficacité diagnostique. De nouvelles techniques projectives ont aussi vu le jour. Comme par le passé, les études consacrées à la psychologie projective concernent essentiellement la psychologie clinique.

Les recherches consacrées aux techniques projectives n'ont occupé qu'une place périphérique dans la psychologie soviétique, elles étaient considérées d'importance mineure. Le progrès dans ce domaine était constamment barré pour des raisons idéologiques. Il y eut par conséquence un véritable hiatus entre théorie et pratique ainsi qu'entre le niveau de la recherche chez nous et à l'étranger. Et pourtant, les techniques projectives entrèrent progressivement dans les pratiques des psychologues grâce aux efforts d'un petit groupe d'enthousiastes. Aujourd'hui les techniques projectives font partie intégrante de la pratique psychologique.

Resumen

Este articulo está dedicado al desarrollo de la investigación en técnicas proyectivas en la psicologia soviética, y resume los estudios proyectivos de la personalidad. Se describen primero los trabajos iniciales con el Rorschach en los años veinte y treinta, previos al periodo de los estudios proyectivos. En los años treinta, las pruebas psicológicas fueron prohibidas como instrumentos para es estudio de la personalidad, debido a sus "perversiones ideológicas" y "concepciones burgueses," y el desarrollo de la psicologia soviética permaneció aislado durante muchos años de los desarrollos exteriores en el mundo de la ciencia.

El proceso de rehabilitación de las pruebas y estudios psicodiagnósticos se inició en los años sesenta, en conexión con los cambios en el clima politico del pais. En ese momento se demostró la utilidad diagnóstica de las técnicas proyectivas en la investigación clínica, y su contribución para identificar caracteristicas de personalidad en los pacientes con trastornos psicológicos en al marco clínico. La investigación clínica consistió inicialmente en especificar indices para diferenciar entre grupos de pacientes en base a sus respuestas al test. También se llevaron a cabo investigaciones teóricas para analizar los conceptos de proyección importandos de otros paises y sugerir enfoques innovadores.

En la década de los ochenta y comienzo de los noventa los estudios teóricos y metodológicos continuaron prosperando. Esta corriente de investigación contemporánea se ha interesado en desarrollar nuevos indices en métodos bien conocidos, mejorar su estandardización y modificarlos para expandir su utilidad diagnóstica. También se han desarrollado varias técnicas proyectivas nuevas. Como en al pasado, el foco principal de los estudios en el campo de la psicología proyectiva continúa siendo la psicología clínica.

La investigación en técnicas proyectivas ocupó un lugar periférico en la psicología soviética y fué considerada como de menor importancia. El progreso en la investigación fué muy frecuentemente restringido por razones ideológicas. Se produjo, como consecuencia, una brecha definitiva entre teoria y práctica, y entre el nivel de la investigación en el país y en el extranjero. Sin embargo, las técnicas proyectivas encontraron gradualmente su camino en el trabajo aplicado de los psicólogos practicantes, gracias al esfuerzo de un pequeño grupo de entusiastas. Hoy en dia, las técnicas proyectivas se han constituido en parte integral de la práctica psicológica.

References

Bespalko, I. G., Gilyasheva, I. N. (1983). Projective technique. In M. M. Kabanov, A. E. Lichko, V. M. Smirnov (Authors), *Methods of psychological diagnostics and correction in clinic* (pp. 116–144). Leningrad: Medicine (in Russian).

Burlatchuk, L. F. (1979). *Personality study in clinical psychology (on the basis of the Rorschach Test)*. Kiev: Zdorovya (in Russian).

Burlatchuk, L. F. (1989a). *Personality psychodiagnostics*. Kiev: Zdorovya (in Russian).

Burlatchuk, L. F., Morozov S. M. (1989b). *Dictionary–reference book on psychological diagnostics*. Kiev: Naukova dumka (in Russian).

Burlatchuk, L. F., Korzhova, E. Yu. (1991). International congresses on Rorschach and other projective techniques. *Questions of Psychology, 4*, 169–173 (in Russian).

Burlatchuk, L. F., Korzhova, E. Yu. (1992). Individual psychological peculiarities in patients with cardiac diseases in the process of their social adaptation. *Psychological Journal, 3,* 112–120 (in Russian).

Burlatchuk, L. F., Korzhova, E. Yu. (1993). On the theory of measured individuality. *Questions of Psychology* (in Russian) (in press).

Sokolova, E. T. (1980). *Projective methods of personality study.* Moscow: The Moscow University Press (in Russian).

Sokolova, E. T. (1987). About the history of projective method. In A. A. Bodalev & V. V. Stolin (Eds.) *General Psychodiagnostics* (pp. 34–45) (in Russian).

Expression of Narcissistic Fantasy in the TAT

Francoise Brelet-Foulard

Université Paris Nord, France

For over 30 years, the French TAT school has used 16 of the 31 cards originally developed by Murray. On the basis of an extensive study of French language protocols, Shentoub identified the most salient perceptual features ("manifest content") and the most frequently cited narrative themes (banal themes). The year 1970 was a turning point for the French school. Using psychoanalytic concepts, Shentoub and Debray (1970) showed that the TAT represents a conflictual situation. More specifically, it captures conflict between two tendencies: a libidinal drive whose expression in fantasy is stimulated by display of the card, and a goal-directedness prompted by the instructions to tell (organize) a story. Thus the TAT situation resonates with affects and unconscious representations evoked by the card, but also invokes communicative requirements and rules of language necessary to relate a story.

The Oedipal fantasy structure is the most economical and efficient way of construing this distinctly human form of conflict, in particular because the TAT situation specifically taps the Oedipal situation in two ways:

1. The scenes in the cards show people interrelating, which orients the subject toward personal fantasy scenarios constructed in the framework of primal fantasies. Elicitation is even more powerful in that the individuals depicted in the drawings (all of the first several cards with the exception of card 3) are clearly differentiated for gender and for generation. Given the order of administration of the cards, the last cards (11, 13B, 13MF, 19, 16)—which are more regressive—enter into this same type of dynamic. Studies of banal themes reinforce this interpretation.

2. The relationship between the psychologist and the respondent, characterized by its asymmetry and by the "seductive" presentation (in the sense of Oedipal maternal seduction) of the cards by the examiner,

also evokes taboo: because there is no dialogue between examiner and subject, the libido can only express itself through narrative construction, as requested in the instructions. However, the instructions themselves are also conflictual. The request to "tell a story that goes with this card" encourages regression and a mode of psychic functioning that is akin to primary processes. At the same time, the instructions call on the subject to channel fantasy into speech that adheres to the secondary process (to the rules of language and its logic). In other words, the libidinal stimulation reactivated by the card in the test situation must be tolerated by the subject, and channeled into a personal form of fantasy. It cannot be drastically repressed and must allow a derivative to emerge. In this way, the unconscious fantasy fuels the creative work required to produce the story. The fantasy is expressed in a sufficiently but not overly distorted form that the Ego can bear and share with others (here the psychologist). All in all, the TAT mimics a situation analogous to everyday behavior.

This analysis of the workings of the TAT led Shentoub to demonstrate that a certain number of sentence construction processes corresponded to defensive behaviors, analogies on an obsessional level, "controlled" processes (A); on the hysterical level, "labile" processes (B); or characterized by inhibition (Cp). (see item coding, mechanisms A, B, Cp, E in the appendix). The role of the psychologist is thus to assess the efficiency of these processes in story construction and in their release of libidinal energy, their power of "disengagement" ("degagement" in Lagache). In this framework, psychotic behavior in the TAT is characterized by a high rigidity of processes, intensification, an inability to restrain the pressure of libidinal needs, and recourse to more archaic modes of functioning (raw fantasies, perceptual distortion, severe speech or thought impairments, etc. termed E processes), which may reveal the type of fantasm at their source.

More recently, a study of projection in the TAT by Brelet (1986, 1987) showed that the notion of "diurnal rest" coined by Freud in 1917, could shed light on the role of the card-as-stimulus in the TAT. In particular, it helps to clarify the ways in which the invitation to tell a story from the card can enable an unconscious wish to be formulated through the material in the card.

Shentoub's interpretative model focuses primarily on neurotic responses and helps identify and grasp disorders and psychotic responses. But the growing number of non-neurotic, non-psychotic disorders has prompted clinicians to take a greater interest in the psychic workings of these types of patients. The Rorschach and the TAT are particularly well suited to these respondents and can help provide more accurate diagnoses.

In 1986, I presented an interpretative model of the TAT based on Shentoub's approach and methodology for studying the non-neurotic, non-psychotic subject. What characterizes these protocols is that they are not structured by the Oedipal fantasy. They may contain stories or episodes indicating hypercathexis in narcissistic fantasies. The discourse structure may show attempts at coping or protecting the individual from being overcome by depressive feelings. The narrative structure may reveal a type of organization, novel forms or a twisting of the thought processes that are adapted to overly active underlying archaic processes, although the meaning and the ability to tell the story remain unaltered.

These protocols were used to define a number of disorders in projective attitude, including wavering and permeability of the boundary between the interpreted space (outside space) and the interpreter's space (inner space), which differ from the confusions found in psychosis. In particular, the model sheds light on borderline states and narcissistic personalities but can also serve to differentiate modes of processing found in addicts, psychopaths, and eating disorder patients. It also lends itself to analysis of thought processes at adolescence and in senescence.

The purpose of this article is to describe certain features of this model through examples of narcissistic case histories. I deliberately do not discuss defensive antidepressive constructions or thought processes "adapted to primary processes and archaic topics" (Anzieu).

Non-Conflictual Narcissistic Narratives

Before discussing these case histories in detail, I first turn to their general features, the most important of which is their non-conflictuality, that is, the lack of psychic conflict between wish and defense.

Poorly placed in time, these secondary traits tend to be frozen moments that have neither beginning nor end. In extreme cases they act as screen images (like screen memories). In these instances respondents may use static verb forms (in French, the infinitive or the present participle) to "suspend" time and elude acknowledging their origins and family ties or any rekindling of a castration fantasy and its obligatory dura-

99

tion in time. The picture is fixed, nonmodifiable, a positive or negative idol for permanent identification.

The use of space and categorization is less distorted than the use of time. The sensory percepts in the card are powerful elicitors. The white, black, and grey areas elicit vivid sensory interpretations—shadows, fog, bright sunshine, snow and its derivatives (cold, hot, etc). These sensory interpretations are the prime means of communicating affect through analogy. These suggestive "atmospheres" help express subjective experiencing and feelings that can be subtle, highly shaded, and often described at length.

In contrast to what is seen in neurosis, these subjects tend to accentuate perceptual features of a hero rather than individuals in interaction. They produce a "one-man show," in which the hero is the only figure that has a prominent place in the story. The other characters are ignored or are secondary, little more than"tokens." The respondent describes mirror-like relationships or provides some other weak elaboration of secondary characters. Often various people in the picture are described as being absolutely identical, so that they exist only as "clones" of the real hero.

It is important to realize that, although the neurotic discourse processes used to construct the story detour from, disguise, or conceal modes of libidinal object cathexis, the stories on this level express features that are closer to unconscious content (once again the issue of an unconscious narcissistic fantasy!). Grandiose narcissistic trends are clearly stated, and when they weaken, more archaic content breaks into the story, such as raw fantasy material and persecutory relationships.

When interpreting, the psychologist is also called upon to deal with what Shentoub termed the "readability" of the story. These stories can be shared and have a communicative value, and the unfolding of the story takes place without much hesitation to produce an account that can be listened to easily. Although some of the stories deviate slightly from the instructions (which call for a story, i.e. having a beginning and an end), they are highly readable and signify good psychic functioning. Other stories are repetitive and full of personal references, a sign of the weakness of narcissistic cathexis and its necessary counterpart in artificial inflation. Ego fragility is apparent, as is its limited ability to fulfill its other functions of reality-testing. The Ego is not distorted as in psychosis, but at times can be highly restricted. The thought processes can undergo pressure from archaic processes, and the maintenance of the boundary between conscious/unconscious may fluctuate, letting unconscious content spill out (note that the border is never broken, as is the case in psychosis).

The Rhetoric of Narcissistic Narrative

The several tendencies that have been mentioned can be observed in the discourse processes that form the architecture of narcissistic stories to the TAT.

Emphasis on Subjective Experiencing (Non-Relational)

The story, as just mentioned, becomes a "one-man show." The self image is erected for purposes of gratification and exhibition to others (in the test setting, the psychologist). This may be done to establish or shore up wavering identification. Sentences in the story may center on subjective experiencing (rather than on interpersonal relationships), and the self-image is described in a nuanced and subtle way. The story exemplifies this experience in a way that specifies and personifies the subject's personality (see Cn 1 on the scoring sheet).

For example, Olivia gave the following story to card 7 GF: "The little girl seems fairly distracted, lost in her dreams, a little abandoned as though she saw something else in her dreams, wrapped up in the dream, she doesn't seem to hear the person talking to her, completely absent, outside. No contact, no, absent, a little sad and bored. So to go on, it's a young girl who is outside reality, can't really adapt, familiar attitude, hard to accept, feels comfortable at home, may be tired of the people around her. She certainly needs lots of tactfulness to be cared for."

Personal or Autobiographical References

Less well elaborated, the story (or episode) in Example 1 below places the respondent in the story: however the projective screen (the story) is not incorporated into the internal space, as in Example 2 below (see Cn2 scoring sheet), where the distance separating the respondent's universe from the narrative universe is no longer maintained.

101

Example 1. Laura to card 1: "I make up a story or I say what it makes me think of? I don't have to make a little speech with a story ... it's hard to tell because it brings things back to me..I can tell you? This little boy makes me think maybe of myself when I was at school. He looks like he is thinking or is bored; that makes me think of me when I had a violin but didn't play it. Music seems to take a lot of his time (...)."

Example 2. Mary to card 5: "It's an old woman who is going into a room looking very surprised, as though she discovered something. *What's funny in the story is that we can see the plot. There's a plot in this story but we don't see it. There are only the woman's eyes to serve as our glasses.* The furniture is fairly ... you get the impression you are in a little girl's room perhaps she has just discovered this young girl with an undesirable person. That's why she is surprised, that's all."

Affect-Title

A short sentence presented as the summary of the next story (like a title to the story) stresses affect, whereas in the neurotic control zone (conflictual stories) there is the same tendency to entitle the story, which however is aimed at distancing the storyteller from affect (see Cn3, scoring sheet).

Example of Laura to card 3BM: "I always want to start by saying what it makes me think of, and not a story. It looks like a child. I'm not sure. Actually it's not a child, it's a woman ... *Disappointment.* A woman crying because she ruined her life."

Narcissistic Details—Self Idealization—Self-Criticism

The next stories contain positive or negative narcissistic details and idealization of the hero. In contrast to neurotic hysteria, the wish to seduce and to be the "snare" are not present. Rather, the purpose is to enhance the self-importance of the hero.

Self criticism (implying that the respondent should never have experienced any failures or difficulties) is also designed to fulfill the same purpose (see Cn9 and Cn10 scoring sheet). Example of Martha to card 5: "*It's a poor spinster, hunched over, narrow-minded, stupid,* who is going to go home. She only takes care of her socks and her cat. Really, *she is completely idiotic.*"

Example of Martha to card 10: "*I don't know, I don't have any imagination, it's always the same. I ruin everything* ... I don't see well. Two old people, two old persons who have gone through life together and have nothing more ahead of them."

Emphasis on Setting Limits and Contours

An emphasis on setting limits and contours is revealed with somewhat different rhetorical forms than in non-conflictual narcissism. The respondent emphasizes everything that draws, bounds, or specifies the contours of the hero of the story. Anzieu's "self-skin" model developed some 10 years ago provides a clinical and theoretical explanation for this type of psychopathological attitude, aimed at maintaining narcissistic confidence. The model stresses boundaries in test responses as metaphors for the boundaries of the self, which are weak in this type of personality. On the Rorschach, work with the barrier and penetration indices has provided evidence of the same type of fragile boundaries (see Cn6 scoring sheet).

Example of Jacques to card 3: "Here is a desolate young man ... *his back is hunched, his clothes are worn out* ... *he is curled up on* the couch. I don't know ... let's say he had a fight with his school mates."

Posture Indicating Affect

Many descriptions of characters in stories focus on posture as a means of communicating affect. In these instances the words describing body position reflect what the hero of the story is experiencing (see Cn4).

Example of Olivia to card 3BM: "... So here ... it looks like a child, rather a teenager. Maybe he is sleeping because he is tired or discouraged, or he is crying, or he fell asleep, I don't know, playing on the ground, he got so tired he fell asleep ... *He is in an abandoned position, more crying than sleeping.* Completely exhausted. He lets everything go, he doesn't have any more strength."

Example of Peter to card 3 BM: "A boy or a little girl. It's not the normal posture for resting, *it's just like the posture of someone who has been rejected.* I, I find that horribly sad. You only show me sad things. It's black and white, more black than white. It's a child who is sad because he got punished and he is waiting for someone to come and comfort him. That's all (?) ... that someone is going to come and talk to him so that he understands what he is being asked, but also why."

Emphasis on Sensory Features

Emphasis on the sensory features of the card, that is, its white, black, and grey values and their contrasts, fulfills the same function as posture in communicating affect. Although descriptive in appearance, the narration focuses on the affective climate of the card and portrays the hero's affects, with this emphasis serving purposes of identification (see Cn5).

Example of Olivia to card 11: "That's strange ... rocks, a stony path. *It's a pointed bridge, more like a mountain landscape, fairly black, bad weather. The walls ... smooth, a feeling of being locked up,* no sky. This part there, clouds and fallen rocks, *fairly closed like an image.* That makes you think of *bad weather, a storm.*"

Depictedness

Another linguistic speech device consists of subjects presenting the scene as objects to be looked at (here by the psychologist). This has been termed "depictedness" (see Cn8).

Example of Camille to card 13B: "There I would say it's a photo, the representation of *a photo, the representation of a photo, which was taken,* and it shows a little boy on the doorstep in a country where it's very hot because you can see a beam of sunlight entering the house, because he's barefoot."

Depictedness is quite similar to an sometimes blends with a form of discourse that deals more with time than with space and is intended less to exhibit oneself to oneself and to others than to locate oneself in time— as if to make time stand still and deny the historical past and future.

Example of Lionel to 7 BM: "That's very beautiful! It's a teacher with a student. It might look like they are playing music, the teacher looks very proud of his student, and sure of himself in his relationship with his student. *It's a momentary vision. I don't see how you can make up a story.*"

104

Mirror Relationships

Finally, referring to mirror relationships allows subjects to find a way of including people whose presence in the card is too obvious to be ignored, but without proposing any object relationship between them. This method of approach in the story-telling is consistent with narcissistic withdrawal (see Cn7).

Example of Camille to card 9 GF. "So there are two women ... who ... two friends or two sisters *because they look a little like each other, who are running, I get the impression that they are in a hurry. They are at the beach*, it looks like there are palm trees."

Another form of this story-telling approach consists of describing two or three people in the card in an identical manner as completely sharing the same identity. Thus the figures in the story may be combined into a single, stereotyped "hero" and become undifferentiated individuals.

Example of Lionel to card 4: "So it's a film set in the 60's. My story is starting off well (laughs). *Two famous American actors*, or a great actor and a great actress, *two big stars who are performing. They are both very beautiful but they* ... there is nothing between them.. She's a bought woman, a prostitute."

Through the disavowal—"there is nothing between them"—Lionel begins to tell a second episode in the story, which this time is conflictual and clearly related to efforts to maintain control.

We can see that the process involved in mirror relationships is not one of confused identity (in which case for a given sentence there would be doubt as to which of two potential subjects should be seen as the subject of the verb). Rather, this telescoping of roles, which is found in the psychotic range, is encountered as well in some hysterical protocols (in which case they involve conflictual stories) and more frequently in borderline protocols. This process occurs fleetingly in narcissistic personalities and indicates the presence of the elaborated narcissistic processes described earlier.

Clinical Interpretation

To be precise, however, the narcissistic rhetoric described in this presentation should be assessed clinically within the dynamics of each individual protocol.

First, it is known that all fantasy scenarios involve both an object polarity and a narcissistic polarity. Let us take as a simple example the statement, "He loves me." The "he" specifies the libidinal object in a relationship of complementarity, and the "me" specifies a "self" in the ordinary sense of the word, which is unique for the other person and as such acquires an identity through this relationship. On the other hand, the narcissistic polarity itself has two facets: a mirror-model, such as the example of the narcissistic woman in Freud's "On Narcissism: An Introduction," who is reflected in the gaze of the man she loves; and the amoeba model, characterized by Freud as the "chief" or "fuhrer" so sure of his "own self" that he needs "no other" to assure his narcissism, in his splendid autocracy.

Overall, then, our primary conclusion is that the narcissistic features of story-telling in the TAT will be normative if the following two conditions are met:

1. Narcissistic features appear only in some parts of the protocol and do not dominate it. The 3BM and the 9GF cards have the strongest pull in this regard, and card 16 (blank), because of its lack of explicit pictorial cues, often gives rise to a story that echoes how subjects represent themselves or their place in the test relationship.
2. Narcissistic features are part of a protocol that is primarily organized around Oedipal concerns. Keep in mind that the stories in this case bear witness to management of libidinal conflict in neurotic terms (wish/defense) in a relationship to another that is cathected and marked by the Oedipal taboo.

In all cases the psychologist needs to identify whether the respondent is producing a story with narcissistic features and which cards prompt this narcissistic cathexis to occur. The psychologist should pay particular attention to the fantasmal overtones generated by Oedipal concerns that create difficulties for the subject. The specific form of fantasy and the card that elicited it can account for narcissistic withdrawal in the face of representations of object relationships carrying an excessively strong countercathexis.

With respect to particular episodes within a story, the psychologist should be attentive to what has preceded the emergence of the episode. More specifically, the dynamic context in which a narcissistic episode appears needs to be defined with care. Was there some defensive lapse or a failure of hysterical or obsessional defenses to resist libidinal pressure? Was this the only way that the subject could handle fantasy content that had become unbearable for the Ego and resulted in the narcissistic thrust breaking through?

The psychologist should also attend to what follows a phase of narcissistic story-telling. Does the subject, in his or her withdrawal, recathect the object polarity elicited by the stimulus card and if so, how? Narcissistic recourse should in this case be viewed as a clinically positive instance of disengagement. Or, in contrast, does the subject become involved in the following kinds of less psychically adaptive or even pathological efforts to manage distress:

1. Elaboration of a story that conveys a more caricatured narcissistic theme, in which the "grandiose Ego" becomes predominant and the thematic content points either to omnipotence or to abject inferiority.
2. Depressive preoccupations that pervade the rest of the story.
3. A change in the direction of the story toward more crude primary process fantasy or persecutory relationships.
4. Increasing recourse to the decor of the card and metaphorical elements that give the story an emotional tone (contrast, isolated perspectives, value of whites, blacks, and grays, etc.), which can leave the subject outside the scope of identificatory supports and trying to compensate for a depletion of object representations (as seen in addictive tendencies and above all food pathologies, some borderline disorders, and certain depressions).

Lastly, the presence of narcissistic phases (like depressive and antidepressive phases) should always be considered carefully in psychotic protocols. These phases are surely positive when they occur in the most pathological protocols, whether they have been moderated through a hypercontrolled relationship to reality, or whether they explode in a "stuck/torn apart/scattered" form of story-telling in which unshareable symbolizations can only barely be restrained. In less severely disturbed protocols, the dynamics of these narcissistic tendencies should also be noted with care. They can give rise to a clinical interpretation similar to the one described in the paragraph above.

Conclusion

The crucial feature of this very brief presentation of narcissistic narrative in the TAT is the following: clinical experience over the last 10 years has clearly shown that discourse processes, which have been isolated here for purposes of presentation, hardly ever emerge in isolation in real protocols. Most of the time, whether they emerge at the same time or in response to other cards, there are a small number of expressions that demonstrate antidepressive defenses, and there are distortions or peculiarities in syntax that signal a thought process that is marked by or tolerant of unconscious processes (primary processes) and more archaic psychic mechanisms, in particular those that are connected to the psychic loci of in/out.

Space prevents me here from elaborating on these fragments of discourse, in particular as regards features relevant to the understanding of borderline states. In any case however, it can be said that modes of managing the psychic economy that demonstrate the expression of narcissistic cathexis in the TAT are to some extent normative and must be predominant to warrant drawing a conclusion of narcissistic personality disorder.

Résumé

La première partie de l'article expose notre système interprétatif, à partir des travaux de l'école française (V. Shentoub, R. Debray). Il exploite le postulat suivant: la fantasmatique du sujet est fortement stimulée par la présentation des planches TAT, qui agissent selon le même modèle que le reste diurne dans la construction du rêve (Freud, 1915—Nouvelles considérations sur le rêve). Cette augmentation de l'excitation pulsionnelle, plus or moins canalisée par le fantasme, trouve son issue dans l'histoire réclamée par la consigne (seul partage permis avec le psychologue dans la situation de test). Aussi le TAT met-il particulièrement à l'épreuve la capacité du fantasme à lier l'excitation pulsionnelle et les modalités de prise en charge de cette fantasmatique par l'activité discursive. V. Shentoub a ainsi mis en évidence des modalités discursives analogues aux modes de fonctionnement névrotiques (hystérique, obsessionnel, phobique) ainsi que leur échecs, la fantasmatique oedipienne apparaissant massivement sollicitée par les planches TAT (R. Debray).

Chez un certain nombre de sujects, la fantasmatique oedipienne n'organise pas le protocole. Les histoires sont cependant "lisibles" (d'une grande capacité à communiquer) et proposent à l'analyse interprétative des modalités discursives tout à fait particulières. C'est ainsi que nous avons pu reconnaître des gestions discursives de l'élaboration fantasmatique qui relèvent du privilègiement du narcissisme ou d'une économie anti-dépressive. Des fonctionnements de pensée–aptes à prendre en charge l'expression de fantasmatiques marquées par l'archaïsme des contenus, et les fonctionnements liés à la fragilité des topiques intrasubjectiges (fonctionnements limites, psychopathies, addictions, pathologies alimentaires, borderline, etc.)–ont pu aussi être mis en évidence, ainsi qu'une pathologie de l'activité projective.

La deuxième partie de l'article proposera l'exemple du maniement discursif favorisant l'expression de la fantasmatique narcissique. L'économie de l'histoire sera différente selon que celle-ci est utilisée comme repli défensif devant la relation objectale ou comme prothèse chez les sujects présentant des difficultés narcissiques graves.

Resumen

La primera parte del artículo expone nuestro sistema interpretivo a partir de los trabajos de la escuela francesca (V. Shentoub, R. Debray). El postulado básico de este enfoque es el siguiente: la presentación de las láminas del TAT constituye en poderosos estímulo a la fantasmática del sujeto, operando de la misma manera que los restos diurnos en la construcción de los sueños (Freud, 1915; Nuevas Consideraciones sobre los Sueños). Este incremento en la excitatión pulsional, canalizado en mayor or menor grado por el fantasma, encuentra salida en la historia requerida por la consigna (único intercambio autorizado con el examinador en la situación de prueba). El TAT pone también a prueba particularmente la capacidad del fantasma en cuanto a ligar la satisfacción pulsional, y las modalidades de asunción de tal fantasmática por medio de la actividad discursiva. En tal sentido, V. Shentoub puso en evidencia modalidades discursivas análogas a los modos de funcionamiento neuróticos (histérico, obsesivo, fóbico), y la forma en que éstas fracasan, momento en el cual la fantasmática edípica es solicitada masivamente por las láminas TAT (R. Debray).

En un cierto número de sujetos, la fantasía edípica no organiza el protocolo. Las historias son sin embargo "leibles" (de una gran capacidad de comunicación) y proponen al análisis interpretativo modalidades discursivas muy particulares. Es así como hemos podido reconocer gestiones discursivas de la elaboración fantasmática que participan de privilegiar el narcisismo o de una economía anti-depresiva. Igualmente, han podido ser puestos en evidencia—al igual que una patología de la actividad proyectiva—modos de functionamiento mental capaces de expresar fantasmáticas marcadas pro el arcaísmo de los contenidos y funcionamientos ligados a la fragilidad de las tópicas intersubjetivas (funcionamiento limite, psicopatías, adicciones, trastornos de la alimentación, borderlines, etc.).

La segunda parte del artículo propondrá el ejemplo del manejo discursivo que favorece la expresión de la fantasmática narcisista. La economía de la historia diferirá en función de si ésta es utilizada como repliegue defensivo ante la relación objetal, o como prótesis en sujetos que presentan dificultades narcisistas severas.

References

Brelet, F. (1986). *Le TAT, fantasme et situation projective*. Paris: Dunod.

Brelet, F. (1987). On cherche un metteur en scene. *Psychologie Francaise, 32,* 137–140.

Freud, S. (1914). Zur Einführung des Narzißmus (On Narcissism: An Introduction). *S.E. XIV,* 67–102.

Freud, S. (1917). Metapsychologische Ergänzung zur Traumlehre (A Metaphyschologcial Supplement to the Theory of Dreams). *S.E. XIV,* 217–235.

Freud, S. (1921). Massenpsychologie und Ich-Analyse (Group Psychology and the Analysis of the Ego). *S.E. XVIII,* 65–143.

Shentoub, V., & Debray, R. (1970). Fondements theoriques du processus TAT. *Bulletin de Psychologie, 24,* 897–903.

Shentoub, V. et al. (1990). *Manuel d'utilisation du TAT, approche psychanalytique*. Paris, Dunod.

UNIVERSITE RENE DESCARTES (Paris V), INSTITUT DE PSYCHOLOGIE, Groupe de Recherches en Psychologie Projective: Manuel d'utilisation du TAT; Approche psychanalytique. Vica Shentoub et al. Paris, Dunod, 1990 (p. 69).

FEUILLE DE DÉPOUILLEMENT

PROCEDES DE LA SERIE A (Contrôle)

A0 Conflictualisation intra-personnelle

A1
1. Histoire construite proche du thème banal.
2. Recours à des références littéraires, culturelles, au rêve.
3. Intégration des références sociales et du sens commun.

A2
1. Description avec attachement aux détails (dont certains rarement évoqués), y compris expressions et postures.
2. Justification des interprétations par ces détails.
3. Précautions verbales.
4. Eloignement temporo-spatial.
5. Précisions chiffrées.
6. Hésitations entre interprétations différentes.
7. Aller et retour entre l'expression pulsionnelle et la défense.
8. Remâchage, rumination.
9. Annulation.
10. Eléments de type formation réactionnelle (propreté, ordre, aide, devoir, économie, etc.).
11. Dénégation.
12. Insistance sur le fictif.
13. Intellectualisation (Abstraction, symbolisation, titre donné à l'histoire en rapport avec le contenu manifeste).
14. Changement brusque de direction dans le cours de l'histoire (accompagné ou non de pause dans le discours).
15. Isolement des éléments ou des personnages.
16. Grand détail et/ou petit détail évoqué et non intégré.
17. Accent porté sur les conflits intra-personnels.
18. Affects exprimés à minima.

PROCEDES DE LA SERIE B (Labilité)

B0 Conflictualisation intra-personnelle

B1
1. Histoire construite autour d'une fantaisie personnelle.
2. Introduction de personnages non figurant sur l'image.
3. Identifications souples et diffusées.
4. Expression verbalisée d'affects nuancés, modulés par le stimulus.

B2
1. Entrée directe dans l'expression.
2. Histoire à rebondissements. Fabulation loin de l'image.
3. Accent porté sur les relations interpersonnelles. Récit en dialogue.
4. Expression verbalisée d'affects forts, ou exagérés.
5. Dramatisation.
6. Représentations contrastées. Alternance entre des états émotionnels opposés.
7. Aller-retour entre des désirs contradictoires. Fin à valeur de réalisation magique du désir.
8. Exclamations, commentaires, digressions, références/appréciations personnelles.
9. Erotisation des relations, prégnance de la thématique sexuelle et/ou symbolisme transparent.
10. Attachement aux détails narcissiques à valence relationnelle.
11. Instabilité dans les identifications. Hésitation sur le sexe et/ou l'âge des personnages.
12. Accent porté sur une thématique du style: aller, courir, dire, fuir, etc.
13. Présence de thèmes de peur, de catastrophe, de vertige etc. dans un contexte dramatisé.

PROCEDES DE LA SERIE C (Évitement du conflit)

C/P
1. Tri long et/ou silences importants intra-récit.
2. Tendance générale à la restriction.
3. Anonymat des personnages.
4. Motifs des conflits non précisés, récits banalisés à outrance, impersonnels, placages.
5. Nécessité de poser des questions. Tendance refus. Refus.
6. Evocation d'éléments anxiogènes suivis ou précédés d'arrêts dans le discours.

C/N
1. Accent porté sur l'éprouvé subjectif (non relationnel).
2. Références personnelles ou autobiographiques.
3. Affect - titre.
4. Posture significative d'affects.
5. Accent mis sur les qualités sensorielles.
6. Insistance sur le repérage des limites et des contours.
7. Relations spéculaires.
8. Mise en tableau.
9. Critiques de Soi.
10. Détails narcissiques. Idéalisation de Soi.

C/M
1. Surinvestissement de la fonction d'étayage de l'objet.
2. Idéalisation de l'objet (valence positive ou négative).
3. Pirouettes, virevoltes.

C/C
1. Agitation motrice. Mimiques et/ou expressions corporelles.
2. Demandes faites au clinicien.
3. Critiques du matériel et/ou de la situation.
4. Ironie, dérision.
5. Clin d'œil au clinicien.

C/F
1. Accrochage au contenu manifeste.
2. Accent porté sur le quotidien, le factuel, l'actuel, le concret.
3. Accent porté sur le faire.
4. Appel à des normes extérieures.
5. Affects de circonstance.

PROCEDES DE LA SERIE E (Emergence en processus primaire)

E
1. Scotomes d'objets manifestes.
2. Perception de détails rares et/ou bizarres.
3. Justifications arbitraires à partir de ces détails.
4. Fausses perceptions.
5. Perception sensorielle.
6. Perception d'objets morcelés (et/ou d'objets détériorés ou de personnages malades, malformés). Fabulation hors image.
7. Inadéquation du thème au stimulus Abstraction, symbolisme hermétique.
8. Expressions „crues" liées à une thématique sexuelle ou aggressive.
9. Expression d'affects et/ou de représentations massifs liés à toute problématique (dont l'incapacité, le dénuement, la réussite mégalomaniaque, la peur, la mort, la destruction, la persécution, etc.).
10. Persévération.
11. Confusion des identités (Télescopage des rôles).
12. Instabilité des objets.
13. Désorganisation des séquences temporelles et/ou spatiales.
14. Perception du mauvais objet, thèmes de persécution.
15. Clivage de l'objet.
16. Recherche arbitraire de l'intentionalité de l'image et/ou des physionomies ou attitudes.
17. Craquées verbales (Troubles de la syntaxe).
18. Associations par contiguïté, par consonnance, coq-à-l'âne.
19. Associations courtes.
20. Vague, indétermination, flou du discours.

The Battery as "Perceptual Hold" in Structural Diagnosis

Helena Lunazzi de Jubany

Universidad Nacional de La Plata, La Plata, Argentina

The proposals put forward in this article were developed for several purposes:

1. To arrive at conclusions that will express the relatively stable configurations of the mental process, with particular attention to the relatively stable organizations that result from the integration and internalization of object relationships. At the same time an attempt will be made to combine structural diagnosis with an idiographic psychodynamic evaluation of the individual.

2. To take account of levels of psychodynamic abstraction that, if sufficiently recognized, make possible the articulation of theoretical notions derived from the information provided by various objective, psychometric, and projective techniques. This approach in turn permits a theoretical formulation of the psychodiagnostic process as a whole.

3. To arrive at an approach that is clear and comprehensive enough to be taught to students of psychology. This approach should allow for linkages between observation and conceptualization and generate conclusions that can readily be understood by psychiatrists and other clinicians. In other words, this purpose consists of facilitating a process of integration between both technical and theoretical considerations and between psychological and metapsychological perspectives, while also taking into account explicit methodological criteria that will assure the status of the psychodiagnostic process as a research endeavor.

In presenting these proposals, we will draw heavily on Schachtel's (1966) rich concept of "perceptual hold" as a way of referring to the battery as a perceptual pillar of structural diagnosis. In addition, to help achieve our aims, we have developed seven connective links between Kernberg's

(1979 a, 1979 b) clinical differentiation criteria and phenomena or indicators in the psychodiagnostic battery (see Table 1): (a) Congruency and (b) Adequacy, which are related to reality testing and thought quality; (c) Identity Representation and (d) Relationships Representations, which are related to the integration of identity and object relations; (e) Primary Repression, which is a barrier function; and (f) Impulse Regulation and (g) Sublimatory Capacity, which are related to defensive operations.

Thus the main headings in Table 1 concern the theoretical level of criteria for clinical differentiation; the secondary headings list the linking concepts that provide psychodiagnostic bridges and describe numerous differential psychodiagnostic indicators. We are currently in the process of assessing the experimental validation of many of the assumptions in this schema and developing research programs concerned with some of them (Lunazzi de Jubany, 1992).

Table 1. Psychodiagnostic linking concepts in structural diagnosis.

Theoretical Level of Criteria for Clinical Differentiation: 1. Reality testing, including sense and perception of reality, and quality of thought processes
Linking Concepts Between Theoretical Level and Indicators
a. Congruence
b. Adequacy

Psychodiagnostic Indicators
a. Congruence expressed with regard to instructions, stimuli, and interpretations; difficulties in congruence are manifest in perceptual distortions, distortions of logic, and errors of space and time orientation.
b. Nature of the quality of thinking as analyzed from the ability to maintain full awareness of impressions formed during both the test administration and interviews; the nature and organization of thought may also be inferred from the adequacy of judgment, the ability to anticipate consequences, and the relative influence of primary and secondary processes.

Theoretical Level of Criteria for Clinical Differentiation: 2. Identity integration and quality of object relations
Linking Concepts Between Theoretical Level and Indicators
c. Identity representation
d. Relationships representation

Psychodiagnostic Indicators
c. Analyzed according to the degree of interpretation achieved, with respect to integration or fragmentation of interpretation of contradictory aspects of representation, conflict, ambivalence, and splitting; also according to the adequacy of level of self-esteem and presence of pathological narcissism

113

Table 1 continued
  d. Nature of the links formed, with respect to whether they are differentiated, symbiotic, or partial and to evidence of integration or non-integration of the superego; also according to they type of object choice, such as anaclitic, narcissistic, etc.

Theoretical Level for Criteria of Clinical Differentiation: 3. Level and quality of defensive operations, including sublimatory capacity
Linking Concepts Between Theoretical Level and Indicators
  e. Primary repression (barrier function)
  f. Impulse regulation
  g. Sublimatory functioning and creativity

Psychodiagnostic Indicators
  e. Presence of censure and pre-repressive or post-repressive operations; attention to flexibility and success of failure of defensive operations; also attention to thematic moderation and the harmony of rational control components versus massive projections, failures, primary thought process phenomena, and inadequate judgment
  f. Capacity to direct and control impulses; capacity to delay in pursuit of goals; capacity to tolerate intense emotions such as anguish, frustration, and losses; capacity to experience and tolerate emotions
  g. Availability of libidinal energy for fantasy and creative work capacity; capacity to participate in collaborative activities; a sense of humor land capacity to enjoy personal achievements and to overcome frustrations; capacity to employ personal resources and experience; capacity to learn from new experiences

---

For many years we have endured considerable skepticism and even discredit regarding the use of psychodiagnostic techniques in my country, Argentina. As we know, similar skepticism and discredit have occurred in other parts of the world, as evidenced in articles by Mahmood (1988) and others. Setting aside for the moment the shifting cycles of interest that characterize professional attitudes, are we as psychologists responsible for this state of affairs regarding the Rorschach? Is it our fault? To attempt an answer to these questions, let us review some potentialities of psychodiagnostic evaluation that may still be scarcely tapped in our professional practice in relation to (a) the effectiveness of assessments, (b) the utilization of psychodiagnostic procedures as meaningful interpersonal situations, and (c) the translation of test findings into appropriate conclusions and recommendations for practice.

We often observe that psychodiagnostic studies fail to answer effectively the questions that have prompted the request for consultation. By "effectively," I mean either drawing conclusions that constitute a reliable and discriminating clinical assessment or operating in a way that leads the consultant through a relevant and significant experience of questioning his or her way of assessing the data. It is in this latter sense that we refer to the psychodiagnostic process as a healthy promoter of change. Unfortunately, however, we have observed little use of psychodiagnosis in this way as an opportunity for promoting healthy change. Moreover, bridges that link conclusions drawn from the evaluation to recommendations for appropriate psychotherapeutic procedures are not well developed. Therefore, the question can be asked whether we are meeting adequately the demands made of us.

Considerable progress has been made in refining our psychodiagnostic techniques. Currently we are able to achieve comprehension of our data in great depth, describing both manifest and latent levels in personality functioning, the balance of regressive pulls and adaptive capacities, sublimatory resources, and the role of symptoms in intrapsychic dynamics.

It is accordingly frustrating to observe, even perhaps absurd, that relying on such a refined and carefully designed technique as the ORT—which is characterized by strict cohesion among the methods of analysis and interpretation—arouses much interest and at times amazement among students and graduates alike as they become familiar with what it can reveal about people, but results in little effective use being made of the technique.

Regarding the Rorschach method as well, we wonder whether the large amount of specialized training required to analyze and interpret it adequately and the effort demanded of the expert who uses it are justified by the frequency of its use and the effectiveness of its results.

As we have stated elsewhere in agreement with Mahmood (1988), "The projectivists should certainly meet the challenges of the 80s and 90s" by updating and streamlining our practices as well as our conclusions and by achieving some epistemological order between theory and technique. Accordingly, it is by modernizing our conceptual framework, adopting broader conceptual notions, and developing more effective ways of answering the questions and meeting the needs of referring persons who request our psychodiagnostic services that we will wear the mantle of healthy change promoters (Lunazzi de Jubany, 1991).

This paper is intended to respond to the need for a broad ordering of psychodiagnostic assessment that will address the grounds on which various therapeutic approaches can be recommended. These comprehensive frames of reference are known in diagnostic terms as "structural diagnosis" (Bergeret, 1983; Kernberg, 1979a) and consist in the inter-

115

pretive process of a shift from "sign" approaches to a configurational study of the relationships among components and the entirety of the discourse structure. All these aspects of the data are to be considered within an interpersonal dynamic framework for psychodiagnostic evaluation, using not merely a test but a selection of techniques called a "battery." Through this approach we can retain the basic psychodiagnostic methodology while also fitting it within the framework of current psychoanalytic formulations.

Rapaport's (1960, 1965) seminal contributions advised psychologists "not merely to use a test but a battery of techniques." But how do we construct a battery, when each technique sheds light—often similar kinds of light—on various levels and organization of psychic functioning? We consider it necessary to pinpoint clinical differentiation criteria to be studied by means of each of the techniques, in different ways and to differing extents. At the same time, these criteria should make it possible to draw broad general conclusions concerning overall psychopathologic personality structures, because the nature of these structures influences which psychotherapeutic approaches are subsequently likely to prove beneficial. Symptom inventories such as the DSM-III-R or OMS tend to emphasize whether the subject meets certain criteria for diagnostic categories without going deeply into his or her unique dynamic, subjective situation. We favor instead integrative approaches based on psychoanalytic perspectives, such as the one developed by Kernberg under the name of "structural diagnosis."

Specifically with respect to considering structural diagnosis, Kernberg (1979 b) says, "It is the one that links the descriptive approach—symptoms and behavior—and the genetic approach—family history—with the understanding of the intrapsychic structural features of the patients." His view represents the psychoanalytic conceptualization of the nature and origin of intrapsychic relationships, which stem from previous internalized relationships and are strengthened, changed, or reactivated within the context of the present interpersonal relationship.

This type of theoretical conceptualization was proposed by Phillipson as the interpretive foundation of his techniques. Kernberg's conceptualization makes more contemporary use of object relations theory, which has been of great help to us (Lunazzi de Jubany, 1991, 1992), because it has allowed us to study the three broad structural personality organizations of neurotic, psychotic, and borderline. These three major structures in turn reflect differences in the functioning of three major criteria clinical differentiation: (a) reality testing, (b) integration of self representation and identity; and (c) developmental level of defense mechanisms (primitive or Oedipal level). In this way, there is a shift away from a narrow focus on diagnostic labels toward attention to the kinds of psychological functioning implied by the labels.

The enriching and significant psychoanalytic developments of recent decades enlighten and guide our understanding of cases, although they might lead us to theoretical eclecticism. The main drawback of eclecticism, in our opinion, is the fact that it dispenses with some widely used and well-known conceptual formulations in order to promote explicitness, adequate application and experimentation, and refutation or confirmation. We believe that Kernberg offers an alternative formulation that is sufficiently consistent to succeed in the difficult task of linking clinical theory and practice.

Method of Case Study

Having these and other auxiliary criteria in mind—such as the depth and stability of inner object relations, ambivalence and tolerance toward love objects, capacity to bear guilt, and degree of self-concept and superego integration—we think that we are prepared to draw comprehensive and justified distinctions between clinical cases. We have gathered data that appear reliable, as judged from sufficient convergence of components throughout the test battery and in interviews as well.

Rather than consider separately the results of the different techniques employed, we need to be able to make inferences based on all of the tests from standpoints reflecting certain levels of "psychodynamic abstraction," which is the classical phrase used by Schafer (1954) when he referred to the thematic analysis of Rorschach contents. The levels of psychodynamic abstraction proposed here are Kernberg's Clinical Differentiation Criteria listed in Table 1, to which we have considered it important to add Bellak's (1968) categories of Creativity, Sublimation, Sense of Humor, and Work Capacity. In analyzing indicators taken from such criteria we can, for example, investigate a certain personality organization by articulating its manifestations in different psychodiagnostic techniques.

In attempting to illustrate with indicators for every criterion, we found that they are not only numerous but also closely related to each other. Putting aside this consideration, which is well known to all of those who

117

work with projective methods, we will illustrate an exploration of some of the main indicators of Identity Organization, arbitrarily selected, though a clinical case named "Purple Rose of Cairo."

In particular, we will examine examples of clinical differentiation criteria (or levels of psychodynamic abstraction), which make it possible to correlate and articulate the conceptual level with the empirical data gathered from techniques. We will exemplify one of these, namely, Identity and Object Relation Organization, in reference to graphic techniques, the Desiderative Technique, the WAIS, thematic techniques (ORT, TAT) and the Rorschach.

We have developed numerous indicators for each clinical differentiation dimension, and it is not possible here to present the complete list. From among the proposed indicators, let us consider the following, dealing with the exploration of Identity Integration.

Selected Indicators of Identity Integration

Graphic Techniques

On graphic techniques, the quality of the drawing stroke can indicate the quality of traits in the subject. The expressive dimensions of intrapsychic states provide an area of contact with the outer world in its spatial grounding. Hence, it is important to observe carefully whatever expressive trends are revealed by the drawing strokes, whether short, neat, straight, continuous or non-continuous, clean or blotted, long, fluid or fragmented, and the like. Special attention should be paid to strokes that emphasize barriers or dynamically significant areas.

Desiderative Technique

On this technique examiners should take note of (a) the distance between idealized dimensions and devaluated dimensions of the chosen objects and (b) the degree and quality of the need to adhere to social conventions as opposed to the degree and quality of the capacity for social originality.

WAIS

On the WAIS, performance on Similarities and Block Design provide indications of dimensions of the articulation of bodily schema and reflect levels of cognitive discrimination referring to differences in self-representation that underlie and articulate identity.

Thematic Techniques (ORT and TAT)

With respect to Identity Integration, thematic techniques should be examined for indices of the capacity to project mediated characters, as opposed to blatant self-projections or clearly self-referential characters. This provides a major clue to whether the subject possesses sufficient integration to maintain identity cohesion and discrimination in interpersonal relationships.

Rorschach

On the Rorschach, M responses associated with H demonstrate the major acquisition of Identity Representational Integration. At least three M in a record of average length signifies achievement of both adequate self-representation and an internal world adequately filled with sublimated human representations. The extent to which this capability is consciously available can be recognized further by the association of M with D locations.

The approach presented here is designed to be accessible to experimentation and validation, even though it has arisen from psychodiagnostic clinical experience gained through 30 years' practice. Similar types of indicators have been devised for the other clinical differentiation criteria of Reality Testing and Thought Processes and Defensive Operations. Our model proposes numerous indicators to be explored. In the assessment of psychopathologic personality structure, it proves useful to corroborate discrepancies or confirmations among the tests against the whole battery of techniques and also the findings from interviews. This procedure allows us to test and evaluate dynamically significant components of personality functioning.

119

Case Study

Let us now turn to the case of Miss O. in order to illustrate our proposed approach. At the time when she was examined, she was 31 years old and engaged in psychoanalytic treatment. After some 7 years of treatment, she had identified herself with the Woody Allen character named Purple Rose of Cairo, and she gave permission for her case to be presented under this name. She continues presently in her treatment.

Miss Purple Rose of Cairo at age 31 is trying to cope with her second university course of study. She first moved from her home of origin to study at the university when she was 18. After about 5 years of studying chemistry, she changed her major area to foreign language. She is now having severe difficulties in concentrating and in expressing herself when she has to write papers, which is a very frequent requirement in her new foreign language area of study. She suffers from severe scoliosis, for which she underwent surgery at age 9 to repair her spinal deviation using three of her own ribs.

Miss O. expresses anger that a man-friend has rejected her, and she lives in a quasi-delusional world in which she creates both pleasant and dramatic love affairs in her fantasy, while in real life she continues to conduct herself as a friendly and devoted woman. She is afraid of having these feelings of unreality, of going crazy or losing control of herself, or of entering into a confusional state. Her family consists of her father, age 50, and a 24-year-old sister; her mother died 3 years previously.

On interview Miss O. shows signs of intense anxiety, suggestive of panic disorder, and seeks professional help in order to be able to complete her current course of study. She reports having many friends and being always pleasant and obedient. She fears that her thoughts and secret forbidden fantasies might emerge in her manifest behavior, or that she may become unable to discriminate between reality and her fantasy world. In particular, she fears that her feelings of unreality could lead to mental unbalance or loss of self-control during a confusional state.

The interview findings suggested that we could be dealing with a severe dissociative identity state or a narcissistic disorder with borderline features. To pursue these possibilities, let us briefly analyze each of the assessment techniques and its indicators.

Graphic Techniques

The subjects reality testing as studied through Graphics Techniques showed clear adequacy and formal congruency and good representations of parts and their relationships. Parts were well discriminated and integrated with correct synthesis. The sequence, length, and placement of figures was coherent. She seemed capable of adequate analysis and critical judgement. Use of manic defense operations was in evidence, as seen in her need of to fill completely the space in the house and scene. She displayed a primitive level of projective identification with little ability to create symbolic mediation. Her defenses appeared to be functioning adaptively.

WAIS

She earned an I. Q. of 130. She showed good analytic and organizing resources, good abstracting and reasoning capability, and very good visual-motor coordination. Her capacities for mediating symbolic space were limited.

ORT

Secondary process thinking was available, but there were areas of omission in her temporal frame of reference. Her stories lacked any reference to past and future events and consisted only of present situations. Her defensive operations consisted mainly of splitting.

Desiderative Technique

There was a preponderance of secondary process thinking. She did use some introductory comments that at times produced shocking and surprising effects, and she showed some rapid shifts in self-referential quality.

Rorschach

She gave 40 responses with an Extended $F+\%$ of 92.5% and 52.2% of $Dd+S$ locations. Her main content themes were photographs, immobilization of living things, and omnipotent control of the inside-outside dimensions.

The high frequency of unusual location choice reflected her excessive need to analyze and verify, deriving support from observational reality while at the same time splitting reality into fragments. The wish is for omnipotent control through an emphasis on exact features and photos. Only once did evidence appear—in Card IV, the response "a burned paper" (*Wv C'F Obj*)—of her denied and rejected self-representation as being fragile and full of holes. This type of experience is typically kept out of her awareness by manic denial, which was also seen in the "house" test, and in other ways in which she revealed intolerance of seeing herself as weak, inadequate, vulnerable, or damaged.

Her denial of impulses and interpersonal interactions was further manifest in representations of parts of figures without bodily content, such as a response of "an open mouth" without reference to the living thing to which the mouth belonged. Finally in this regard, there were many responses involving immobilized figures, such as to card X, "Yellow lions in the position of a statue." This recourse to immobilization reflected her wish to control life, both internally and external to herself, in an omnipotent fashion.

Other Rorschach findings significant for her relationships include the following: $H+A:Hd+Ad$ = 18:18; six M—one each on Cards I, III, V, and VII and two on Card IX—of which five involved H and one Hd content; and eight FM and four $Fm+mF$, including one in which the figure has "suffered."

Thus splitting and manic denial appear as the main defensive operations. There is severe impairment of creativity (W = 12%). The adaptive functions of the ego are well-maintained, and some potential resources are suggested by many original ($O+$ and $O-$) responses. In summary, she shows a good level of secondary process thinking but considerable stress revealed by use of primitive defense mechanisms, in particular, prominent splitting and breakdowns in repressive functioning. The diagnostic conclusion is borderline personality organization.

Conclusion

This concludes a selective journey through some indicators of personality functioning in our model. We need to emphasize several points, however.

1. The differential clinical criteria and their indicators have been discussed separately only for didactic purposes. In actual practice, it is very important for interpreters to conduct a configurational and simultaneous analysis of them.
2. The theoretical meaning of the various clinical differentiation criteria goes well beyond the possibilities that could be delineated in this paper and that play a necessary part in a thorough assessment of the psychodiagnostic indicators. Readers are referred in this regard to the basic sources listed in the bibliography.
3. The indicators that have been mentioned do not begin to encompass the full range and complexity of indicators that can be applied in a clinical case study, but they do present an ample repertory to guide study of the criteria.
4. The indicators proposed do not replace the interpretive rules and guidelines of the individual psychodiagnostic techniques. They constitute instead a structured approach to configurational evaluation of the import of the data to be conducted after the traditional analysis of the component tests in the battery has been completed.

The methodological process for psychodiagnosis that we have developed consists of a five-step investigation: (a) analysis of the interview and formulation of hypotheses to be explored; (b) analysis of the individual techniques in the test battery one at a time to identify consistent findings within each of them; (c) analysis of the test battery as a whole in order to identify consistent findings across the individual tests; (d) confirmation or rejection of the hypotheses being explored; and (e) structural diagnosis as suggested by the proposed indicators based on the selected clinical differentiation criteria with which we work.

Despite being able to illustrate only a small portion of our proposal, we hope that the reader will be able to grasp the sense of these indicators as they may uniquely appear in each case. We hope further to achieve through presenting our theoretical and technical approach a common frame of reference for working in collaboration with other psychologists. We have developed numerous indicators as well as various guidelines for clinical judgment in the psychodiagnostic process. We do not wish to promote any particular categorical judgments or conclusions, but we do want psychodiagnosis to proceed in an objective manner based in a clear convergence of multiple indicators appearing throughout an entire test battery.

Résumé

Nous proposons ici de considérer la batterie de test dans son ensemble comme un pilier de la "mainmise perceptive" du processus de psychodiagnostic. Le concept de "mainmise perceptive" a été élaboré par Schachtel pour enrichir notre compréhension de la réponse formelle au Rorschach, mais elle peut aussi servir à souligner l'importance de la batterie entière dans un processus d'évaluation.

Nous proposons d'établir des liens entre niveaux théorique et d'observation et un répertoire d'indicateurs aux tests qui doivent être analysés à travers une approche configurationnelle du psychodiagnostic qui implique la prise en compte de toute la batterie. Les aspects théoriques de notre travail utilisent les critères décrits par Kernberg pour la clinique différentielle du diagnostic de structure. Nous insistons aussi sur l'évaluation des capacités de créativité, du sens de l'humour, du plaisir, ainsi que sur quelques unes des notions fondamentales de la psychologie du moi et des fonctions du moi telles que développées par Bellak.

Notre travail s'inscrit dans le souci de répondre aux besoins de l'enseignement et de la pratique du psychodiagnostic, et vise à résoudre des difficultés qui sont apparues au cours de 25 ans de fréquentation des techniques projectives. Tout d'abord, nous devons disposer de concepts théoriques qui nous permettront d'articuler les différents niveaux d'information concernant les processus psychiques qui nous sont fournis par les différentes techniques psychologiques. Ces concepts devraient englober des dimensions à la fois psychologiques et métapsychologiques du fonctionnement de la personnalité.

En deuxième lieu, dans la pratique du psychodiagnostic, nous devons ordonner les informations de bases, mais néanmoins profondes, qui établissent les critères diagnostiques et nous permettent de poser des indications thérapeutiques pertinentes. Ordonner ces informations implique d'obtenir des évaluations qui ne soient pas uniquement centrées sur la nosographie mais qui tiennent aussi compte du potentiel adaptatif des sujets, du sens que prend leurs symptômes dans leur histoire, et du degré d'organisation de leur identité. C'est pourquoi nous nous intéressons à des approches psychodiagnostiques qui rendraient compte de l'organisation structurale des processus stables de la personnalité et qui, en même temps, seraient sensibles à la singularité et à la complexité de la dynamique personnelle originale.

En troisième lieu, et également important, nous devons nous soucier de (a) élaborer une méthodologie de psychodiagnostic qui soit claire dans sa théorie et dans ses techniques afin de pouvoir être enseignée à des étudiants qui apprendront à penser de manière logique et à introduire la créativité dans leurs évaluations tout en étant capable de traiter et organiser les informations qu'ils obtiennent; (b) améliorer la fiabilité du jugement clinique par l'étude des phénomènes récurrents tant à l'intérieur d'un même test que entre les tests tout en ne négligeant pas l'exploration du pourquoi et comment ces données apparaissent; (c) démontrer l'utilité du psychodiagnostic en tant qu'un instrument pour penser de manière clinique les expériences de vie; et (d) travailler avec une méthodologie de psychodiagnostic qui non seulement produise des jugements cliniques fiables mais les exprime dans des conclusions qui soient compréhensibles par d'autres professionnels.

Les psychologues doivent pouvoir exprimer leurs résultats de manière claire, et c'est dans ce but que nous avons élaboré notre projet qui devrait aider les examinateurs à penser et à élaborer les données. Plus nous nous rapprocherons de formulations claires et fiables, et plus nous démontrerons la validité et l'efficacité des procédures de psychodiagnostic. Il est important de se rappeler que notre proposition, que nous illustrons par un bref cas clinique, consiste en un effort d'organisation. Nous présentons des listes d'indicateurs à rechercher dans les différentes techniques mais seulement après que l'on ait formulé des hypothèses au cours des entretiens et de l'interprétation individuelle des tests. Nous voulons parler de l'analyse des indicateurs récurrents dans l'ensemble de la batterie.

En conclusion, nous considérons le processus de psychodiagnostique comme un élément de recherche, qui commence avec des hypothèses formulées lors des entretiens et qui se développe à travers différentes techniques. La dernière étape consiste à organiser l'ensemble de l'information en fonction des critères de différenciation clinique et de leurs indicateurs proposés, en utilisant la batterie pour confirmer ou infirmer les hypothèses initiales.

Resumen

En este trabajo la Batería Psicodiagnóstica en su conjunto se propone como pilar o "perceptual hold" del proceso psicodiagnóstico. El concepto "perceptual hold" fue elaborado por E. Schachtel para la interpretación de las respuestas de Form en Rorschach. Sin embargo, est artículo propone que el concepto pueda también ser empleado para enfatizar el lugar de la Batería en el proceso de evaluación.

Con el objeto de llegar al arriba mencionado objetivo, lo que se sugiere son nociones articuladores psicodiagnósticas y un amplio repertorio de indicadores a ser analizados utilizando en enfoque configuracional; estas nociones han de ser estudiadas utilizando el conjunto de la Batería. Los criterios de Diferenciación Clínica de Diagnóstico Estructural de O. Kernberg son utilizadas en un nivel teórico. La evaluación de la Creatividad, Capacidad de Humor, Goce y Trabajo son enfatizadas, incluyendo también nociones fundamentales de la Psicología de Yo y los desarrollos de L. Bellak.

Las necesidades surgidas tanto en la enseñanza del Psicodiagnóstico come en la aplicación y también en el consecuente trabajo de intercambio con colegas han dado lugar a la elaboración de este trabajo. Consiste en una propuesta de resolución de dificultades vivenciadas a lo largo del ejercicio del enfoque proyective durante más de veinticinco años.

1. Nivel teórico: Une de las necesidades primordiales se sitúa en el logro de nociones teóricas que permitan la articulación con los distintos niveles de procesos psiquicos disponibles en Técnicas Psicodiagnósticas disimiles. Estas nociones han de poder responder tant a dimensiones Metapsicolólogicas como Psicológicas.

2. Una segunda y muy importante necesidad relacionada as empleo del psicodiagnóstico es ofrecer información esencial, sin embargo profunda, para establecer criterios; este procedimiento nos permitirá planear estrategias psicoterapéuticas potenciales. Este método requiere que se obtengan evaluaciones que, sin estar necesariamente centradas alrededor de la nosografía, peudan dar cuenta del potencial de salud, el sentido del sintoma en la historia personal y el grade de organización de la indentidad. Entonces, nos referimos a enforques psychodiagnósticos que den cuenta de la organizacióon relativamente estable de los procesos mentales, cristalizando estructuras y, al mismo tiempo, sensibles a la uniquidad y complejidad del enfoque idiosincrásico.

3. Tercero, pero igualmente importante, la necesidad de apuntar hacia:

a. Una metodología psicodiagnóstica teórica y técnicamente ordenada a ser enseñada al estudiante, quien es estimulado a pensar, a incorporar creatividad en su evaluación y, a la vez, a ordenar y manejar la información obtenida.

b. La confiabilidad de los Juicios Clínicos y su validez es salvaguardada a través de la aplicación del estudio de recurrencia de información intra e intertest. Se trata, sin embargo, de no descuidar la exporación de preguntas del Como? y del Por qué?

c. Apuntamos a mostrar el Psicodiagnóstico a los estudiantes de Psicología como una herramienta para pensar tanto los fenómenos Clínicos como los de la vida cotidiana.

d. Una metodoligía Psicodiagnstico no sólodirigida a realizar Juicios Clínicos sonfiables pero también a expresarlos en una conclusión entendible por la interdisciplina (Jueces, Empleadores, Clínicos, Psiquiatras, etc.). El Psicólogo necesita expresar los resultados de manera clara; pensando y elaboando datos, esta propuesta trata de ayudarlo a lograr ese objetivo. Más cerca nos encontremos de la formulación de conclusiones confiables y claras, más próximos también a probar la validez y eficacia de los procedimientos psicodiagnósticos.

Es importante recordar que la presente propuesta, que es brevemente ejemplificada con un caso clínico, consiste en un esfuerzo organizativo. A pesar de que se ofrecen listas de indicadores a ser leídas en distintas técnicas, estas listas deben ser consultadas no antes sino después de: (a) la formulación de una hipótesis durante las entrevistas; (b) la evaluación técnica por técnica. Esto significa que nos refermimos al análisis de la recurrencia de indicadores en la batería completa después de investigar el Como?, el Por qué? y el Del qué peude tratarse?

En conclusión, subyace a este trabajo una concepción del proceso psidiagnóstico como mini investigación; esta fue desencadenada a partir de hipótesis obtenidas en entrevistas y sucedida por una exploración técnica pro técnica. Por último ordenaremos la información según criterios de Diferenciación Clínica y los respectivos indicadores sugeridos. Las Batería dará apoyo o refutará la hipótesis inicial.

References

Bellak, L. (1968). *Ego function assessment* (A Manual). C.P.S.

Bergeret, J. (1983). *Personalidad normal y pathologica*. Mexico City: Editoral Gedisa.

Kernberg, O. (1979a). *La teoria de las relaciones objetales y el psicoanalisis clinico*. Buenos Aires: Editorial Paidos.

Kernberg, O. (1979b). *Desordenes fronterizos y narcisismo patologico*. Buenos Aires: Editorial Paidos.

Lunazzi de Jubany, H. (1991). La technique des relations objectales de H. Phillipson dans le diagnostic de structure. *Bulletin de la Societe du Rorschach et des Methodes Projectives de Langue Francaise, 35*, 105–116.

Lunazzi de Jubany, H. (1992). *Lectura del psicodiagnostico*. Buenos Aires: Editorial de Belgrano.

Mahmood, Z. (1988). The projective scene in the world at large: A blot on the landscape. *British Journal of Projective Psychology, 33*, 54–66.

Rapaport, D. (1960). Implications teoricas de los procedimientos de verification diagnostic y las tecnicas proyectivas y la teoria del pensar. In R. Knight (Ed.), *Psiquiatria psicoanalitica*. Buenos Aires: Editorial Horme.

Rapaport, D. (1965). *Test de diagnostic psicologico*. Buenos Aires: Editorial Paidos.

Schachtel, E. (1966). *Experiential foundations of Rorschach's test*. London: Tavistock Publications.

Schafer, R. (1954). *Psychoanalytic interpretation in Rorschach testing*. New York: Grune & Stratton

Some Contributions of Cognitive Science to the Rorschach Test

Marvin W. Acklin

Honolulu, Hawaii, USA

Now over seventy years old, the Rorschach Test has achieved unprecedented visibility and utilization in clinical psychology. After a decade of criticism and predictions about the demise of projective testing in general, the test remains widely used and investigated. This resurgent trend seems largely attributable to the work of John E. Exner, Jr., whose *Comprehensive System for the Rorschach* (1986, 1991) placed the test on a solid psychometric footing. Aside from the massive efforts to establish reliability and validity data for the various determinants, ratios, and percentages, Exner has more recently turned his attention toward interpretive strategies which integrate the complex data of the structural summary (Exner, 1991).

A second trend in the resurgence of the test is undoubtedly related to developments in psychoanalytic theory. Developments in clinical psychoanalysis since the mid '70's, with their focus on experience-near conceptualization, rejection of metapsychology, and increasing affinity for empirical approaches, have made a significant contribution to the test's application and general level of interest. Contemporary efforts in integrating psychometric/nomothetic data with theory saturated idiographic/content-based information are becoming a trend and commonplace (Erdberg, 1993).

Exner's approach to the test, with its empirical focus, has been the target of the criticism that his atheoretical emphasis is reductionistic, atomistic, and most importantly, obscures the richness and depth that theory brings to both the interpretive process and an understanding of the processes that underlie test determinants and structural data. Exner's recent interests in cluster analysis, while leaning toward a view of the data from the structural summary as reflecting integrated processes, have fallen short of a more thorough-going integration of processes, scores, and structural data.

Without entering into the empirical versus theoretical debate, it suffices to say that the test, as a clinical technique which taps into complex cognitive processes, is able to accommodate various conceptual and theoretical frameworks. While theory undoubtedly enriches Rorschach psychology, the beauty of the test is that it is *not* inherently wedded to a particular theoretical outlook or framework. As anyone acquainted with the history of science will attest, conceptual frameworks emerge and disappear with common frequency. Rorschach's seminal contribution (1969) reflected the atheoretical and classification approach of Kraepelinian psychiatry of the later nineteenth century. Later conceptualizations have been framed into psychoanalytic drive, ego, and object relations frameworks. While no theoretical framework is likely to be exhaustive and the last word, emergent paradigms have the value of casting old or outmoded concepts into a new language. The current contribution highlights emerging models from cognitive science (Stein & Young, 1992).

Centrality of the Response Process

Despite the emphasis placed on the psychometric respectability of the Rorschach that has predominated during the past two decades, the core of the test and its most profound contribution to understanding the functioning of people is found in the interval between the presentation of the cards with the instruction, "What might this be?," and the subject's verbalization. There is, in clinical work, perhaps no more fertile and promising interval for understanding the complex and subtle workings of the brain and mind. This, the response process, is the very heart and soul of the Rorschach Test. No deep mastery of the test is possible without an understanding of what is happening between the presentation of the cards and the verbalization.

Rorschach offered little elaboration of the processes underlying responses to the cards beyond a pregnant, and still highly applicable quote from his mentor Bleuler, couched in terms of associationist psychology:

Perceptions arise from the fact that sensations, or groups of sensations, ecphorize in us a complex of memories of sensations, the elements of which, by virtue of their simultaneous occurrence in former experiences, have a particularly fine coherence and are differentiated from other groups of sensations. In perception, therefore, we have three processes: sensation, memory, and association. This identification of a homogeneous group of sensations with previously acquired analogous complexes, together with all their components, we designate as apperception (Rorschach, 1969, pp. 2–3).

A number of later treatments of the response process (Rapaport, Gill, & Schafer, 1968; Schafer, 1954; Exner, 1989, 1991; Gold, 1987; Acklin, 1991) have attempted to elucidate what happens after the examinee is handed the cards. These will not be reviewed here. Rorschach's quote of Bleuler places the response process into the context of associationist psychology. Rapaport understood the response process as a dialectic between association and perception reflecting the influence of ego psychology. Schafer's view of the response process viewed it on a continuum of psychic functioning intermediate between dream states and waking consciousness, again reflecting the theoretical tenets of psychoanalytic psychology. Exner, in characteristic fashion, eschewed theoretical constructs in his formulation, focusing more on surface, conscious, and volitional processes. Acklin applied developments from contemporary cognitive and developmental psychology, using resources from Horowitz (1988) and Stern (1985). The current contribution is an elaboration of these notions by integrating two powerful trends in contemporary American psychology: schema theory and information processing approaches. After brief reviews of these developments, a contemporary reformulation of the response process will be proposed.

Schema Theory

While the schema construct has been around for over sixty years (Bartlett, 1932), it has only recently become the basis for widespread research and clinical application. Schemas may be defined as generic knowledge structures, having reference to self, relational transactions, and situations. They are essentially "prototypes which are constructed anew for each occasion by combining past experiences with their biases and activation levels resulting from the current experience and the context in which it occurs" (Norman, 1986). These internalized representations are thought to serve as organizers of perception, cognition, emotion, and action as they are activated or instantiated by situational triggers. As precipitates of lived experience, schematic structures are prototypes which form the representational substrate of interpersonal experience and behavior. Schemas, as we shall see below, are not static "engrams"

131

that are localized but may best be thought of as organized into dynamic networks with complex systems of activation, inhibition, control, and compromise expression. Schemas are developmentally acquired through experience, that is, they are encoded and reworked across developmental stages described Stern (1985) under cognitive and perceptual rules which organize the encoding and assimilation of experience. Through lived experience and developmental maturation in the context of the average expectable environment, schemas are gradually reworked into age appropriate templates for social perception and interaction (Baldwin, 1992). Schemas which are instantiated by situational inputs from the environment form "working models" of ongoing experience which more or less demonstrate goodness of fit. Obviously, the degree of goodness of fit will have much to do with adaptive success or failure. Working models, based as they are on schematic infrastructures may be progressive, adaptive, and mature, or they may be regressive, maladaptive, and immature. As mature, they tend to be reality based and accurate. As immature or regressive, they may reflect associations, representations, and emotional experiences from earlier situations and developmental stages. Schematic processes function unconsciously and in parallel forms in the construction of working models, a point that will be pursued below in the discussion of models of information processing.

Figure 1 depicts the relations between schemas and the organization and regulation of working models in the context of ongoing social interaction. One schema may "dominate the template of the working model as shown by the heavy arrow. Enduring schemas of a type may also have layers of more progressive or regressive forms as shown by the overlapping small boxes" (Horowitz, 1989, p. 261).

In contrast to the two dimensional surface model depicted in the upper part of Figure 1, the lower part of Figure 1 depicts the same self-other schema (otherwise known as an object relation) along developmental or epigenetic lines (Emde, 1988a, 1988b). The developmental precursors of contemporary schemas or self, others, and situations bear a close resemblance to Erikson's epigenesis, "newer developmental versions of a given type of interpersonal situation stacked on top of earlier schemas" (Horowitz, 1991). The inner checking along the developmental axis represents the affective core of the schema.

Schemas are internalized, dynamic knowledge structures which organize perception, cognition, emotion, and action in social interactions. As constantly shifting working models, they represent "ego states" or "states of mind" (Horowitz, 1987; Horowitz, Fridhandler, & Stinson, 1991)

Marvin W. Acklin

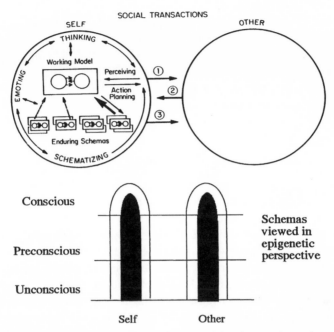

Figure 1. Model of a social transaction demonstrating interactive, schematic, and epigenetic dimensions.

which are experiential correlates of instantiated schemas. Schemas, as role-relationship models (Horowitz, 1989) tend to be parallel processed to provide the best fit possible, given the constraints of their properties and the demands of the external situation. They are prone to progressive or regressive shifts according to their structural organization and situational demands. Several working models may be instantiated simultaneously in complex or ambiguous situations, representing an inherently unstable balance of controls and defenses.

Schema theory provides a useful heuristic framework for illuminating aspects of the Rorschach response process that are obscured in black box models presented by theorists as Rapaport and Exner. Schematic processing is multidimensional, having surface, transactional, and developmental-epigenetic dimensions. In this context, schemas are processed interactively and multiply. This framework renders a number of academic debates about primary versus secondary process, conscious versus unconscious cognition, and projection versus classification, because schematic processing occurs interactively, simultaneously, at multiple organizational levels, only some of which are accessible to conscious rep-

133

resentation (Horowitz, 1988). After discussing information processing models derived from contemporary cognitive psychology, including the sequential symbolic, and connectionist or parallel distributed processing models, and the integration of schema theory into this framework, we shall be in the position to apply these propositions to a reformulation of the Rorschach response process.

Information Processing Approaches

A second paradigm that has become well established in American experimental psychology and is making its influence felt in clinical psychology is the "information processing" approach (Palmer & Kimchi, 1986). Information-processing analyses characterize human cognition as a series of stages, or transformations, between stimulus input and response output (Greenwald, 1992). Quoting Ingram and Kendall, the paradigm conceptualizes the person as an information processing system and focuses largely upon the structures and operations within the system and how they function in the selection, transformation, encoding, storage, retrieval, and generation of information and behavior (1986, p.5).

The reader cannot fail to note the potential applications of information processing approaches to Rorschach psychology. Within the information processing paradigm, analogies were made early between mental processes and those of a digital computer. Currently, cognitive architecture is specified typically in either symbolic or connectionist terms (Stein, 1992). Symbolic systems includes levels of processing models, spreading activation models, and schema approaches. The components of connectionist approaches are based on an abstraction of our current understanding of the information processing properties of neurons (Feldman & Ballard, 1982).

The "sequential symbolic" paradigm (SSP; Newell & Simon, 1965) or "symbolic" paradigm (Smolensky, 1986, 1988) dominated the field of cognitive psychology for almost three decades. Figure 2 depicts a typical symbolic model of mental processes.

Despite the gains accrued through the advent and spread of symbolic and computational models for mental processes, including the foundation of the field of artificial intelligence, it has become increasingly clear that the symbolic models are inadequate for explaining complex pro-

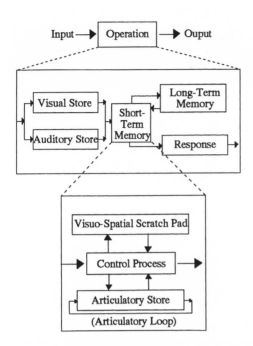

Figure 2. Schematized depiction of a serial model of information processing.

cesses involving simultaneous consideration of many pieces of information or constraints.

> The basic tenets of information processing theory characterize mental events as abstract and discrete representations processed by sequential processes of symbolic manipulation. This view is challenged by the connectionist approach which conceptualizes mental events as the products of a distributed representation manipulated with largely continuous and simultaneous processing performed by numerous very simple, but densely interconnected elements (Caspar, Rothenfluh, & Segal, 1992).

Parallel distributed processing models have been proposed as an alternative to serial models of cognition. These models attempt to model mental processes in terms approximating functioning in neural networks.

Early attempts in developing neurally-based cognitive models of information processing were advanced (Rosenblatt, 1962), but it has only been in the past five or ten years that they have achieved dominance in the field. Parallel distributed processing (PDP) or connectionist models of human cognition challenge the notion that the digital computer provides the best analogy for the working of the human brain and mind.

Instead of the computer metaphor for cognition, the PDP model proposes a brain metaphor, that is, that mental processes are better conceived as occurring in "large dynamic networks consisting of simple neuron-like processing units" (Stinson & Palmer, 1992, p. 345).

Connectionist models describe the microstructure of cognition in terms of densely interconnected computing elements (called units) in relation to one another (connections) in complex patterns (networks). Units are activated according to connection strengths (weights) which activate or inhibit network connections (represented in Figure 3 by weighted coefficients). Networks are organized into collections of units organized as layers. Hidden units or layers of units may have neither input or output connections, but are solely connected within the network. "In systems with hidden layers, incoming information is recoded in the hidden layers into an internal representation and the outputs are generated from the internal representation instead of the original pattern (as encoded by the input layer)" (Caspar, Rothenfluh, & Segal, 1992, p. 722). Information is processed by the propagation of activation and inhibition in the network.

In this framework, processing is massively parallel, distributed, and representations, rather than being localized are conceived as fields of activation and inhibition within a neural matrix with the goals of maximal constraint satisfaction (Rumelhart, Smolensky, McClelland, & Hin-

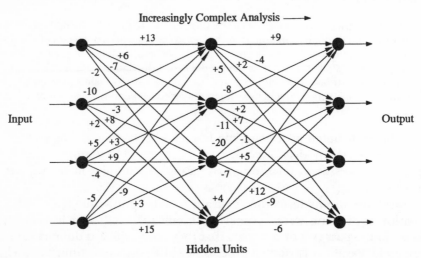

Figure 3. Schematic representation of a connectionist network model for information processing.

ton, 1986). Knowledge is not stored in a locale or even in the connections of a special unit reserved for that knowledge, but is distributed over the connections among a large number of processing units (McClelland, Rumelhart, & Hinton, 1986). In contrast to sequential paradigms, the PDP approach is based on the concept of "distributed representations" (concepts, including memories are stored as global patterns of activation over many units of the network), recurrent feedback loops, including feed forward and feed backward processes, that most closely satisfy the nature of the information from the environment and the structural constraints built into the network, and "learning algorithms" that allow networks to learn automatically how to map input activations onto outputs by adjusting the activation weights on connections between units in complex nets (Stinson & Hinton, 1991).

Parallel distributed processing models may not entirely address issues related to human cognition, for example, there are clear sequential processes in thinking. Controversies about the relations between microstructural and macrostructural processes in cognition and their link to sequential or distributed processing have emerged (Fodor & Pylyshyn, 1988). In this case, hybrid approaches combining sequential and parallel distributed models are emerging (Casper, Rothenfluh, & Segal, 1992; Norman, 1986).

While this preliminary overview cannot do justice to the complexity and potential applications of information approaches, especially PDP, its application to Rorschach psychology cannot be overlooked, as the next section of this discussion will attempt to make clear.

The Rorschach Response Process: A Reformulation

Serious consideration of the Rorschach response process inevitably involves appreciating the context of responding (Phillips & Smith, 1954; Schafer, 1954; Schachtel, 1966). In most cases this is an evaluation situation, typically involving questions related to mental health. The evaluation context, defined by Schachtel as the examinee's "subjective definition" of the situation, forms a supraordinate schema (Horowitz, 1988) into which multiple, subsequent perceptions and behaviors in the testing situation are framed. The testing situation schema is dynamic and mercurial, contributed to by the expectations, past experiences, and potential consequences of the evaluation, on the examinee's part, the setting, stimulus qualities, and interpersonal skills of the evaluator, and the un-

137

certainties of the ongoing process between them. The testing schema's supraordinate status is not inconsequential. Research has shown significant gender effects, for example (Greenberg & Gordon, 1983). Research has also demonstrated the powerful impact of instructions and prior familiarity with the examiner on response productivity (Berger, 1954; Exner, 1986; Gibby, 1952; I.B. Weiner, Rorschach Workshop notes, December 1983).

The instructions for the association phase of the test make a significant contribution to the examinee's evaluation schema, couched as they are in "what if" terms of the subjunctive mood ("What might this be?"). The subjunctive mood occupies a space mid-way between factual reality (Rapaport's perception) and inner fantasy (Rapaport's association). The indefiniteness of the instructions and the "potential space" (Smith, 1990) created thereby confronts the examinee with considerable ambiguity. Association phase instructions create relatively loose constraints on the procedure.

Presentation of the first card involves an encounter with a fairly complex, but unfamiliar stimulus which prompts visual scanning and encoding, initiating the response process proper. Tachistoscopic presentation of Rorschach cards indicates that multiple responses are possible in extremely brief exposures (less than one second; Colligan & Exner, 1985, 1986). Thus, the encoding and processing of the blot occurs in very short periods of time. Through encoding of the blot, a process of multiple schematic instantiation or activation occurs, probably best thought of as a network stored in long-term memory. The rapidity of this process can best be explained in terms of distributed and parallel processing. Undoubtedly, the novelty of the blots themselves further contributes to the potential space providing a container, as it were, wherein multiple schematic instantiations are possible.

This process of multiple schematic activation and sorting represents the heart of the response process. Activated schemas are managed through defensive control processes (otherwise known as ego defense mechanisms) which—through selection of content, control of form of representing and sequencing of ideas, images, and feelings, and control of repertoires of schemas—ward off or transform feared schemas or those that conflict with desired schemas (Horowitz, Cooper, Fridhandler, Bond, & Vaillant, 1992). The nature and quality of this process provides a most unique source of information in understanding the examinee's inner organization and experience and forms a critical foundation for the diagnostic task. The constraints imposed by the stimulus

(Exner, 1991), the nature, range, and quality of instantiated schemas, including the flexibility and adaptiveness of the control processes all converge upon a suitable compromise, the verbalization. Real-time processes of schema activation and inhibition are linked to internal ego states, derived from shifting working models. When schemas are multiply activated or in competition with one another, "shimmering states" (Horowitz, 1991, p. 23) occur and may be noted in the behavior of the examinee, including intrusive thoughts or affects, verbal asides, or lapses in concentration. Horowitz notes, with respect to shimmering states that

> there is less coherence of signs and signals in such shimmering states, for their features are composites of different schemas. During shimmering states of mind different features may leak through each other, rapidly exist, desist, and reappear, or else lead to discordant verbal and nonverbal message. (Horowitz, 1991, p. 24)

It is not uncommon to observe a convergent process between test behavior, the verbalization, and the score (Schafer, 1954), a situation in which the examiner can place the greatest diagnostic confidence.

The outcome of this process is, of course, the verbalization, which represents a compromise end product which residualizes the various forces. This situation neatly fits the notion of "constraint satisfaction" in a neural network where a state of settling or relaxation occurs after the achievement of an optimal fit in which as many constraints as possible are satisfied (Rumelhart, Smolensky, McClelland, & Hinton, 1986). All of this occurs, it should be recalled, in the presentation of the first card.

In other words, the process of taking the Rorschach involves the activation and sorting of schemas and their associated phenomenological affective correlates in the context of a somewhat ambiguous, what-if type of situation. The ambiguity of the instructions and the novelty of the cards, provokes a rich container for schematic activation and processing. Through feedback loops, working models are fluidly activated, sorted, and inhibited as sources and constraints of affect, perception, and test behavior, including the verbalization, within the constraints of the stimulus properties of the card and the working model of the evaluation situation. The verbal response represents, in PDP language, the convergence of the activated neural network toward a state that "maximizes a global measure of goodness of fit or degree of constraint satisfaction" (Rumelhart, Smolensky, McClelland, & Hinton, 1986). This whole dynamic process, occurring in seconds or milliseconds, is ultimately residualized as a code or "score."

This, of course, is not the end of the test. The examinee is presented with another card which reengages the whole process. The previous verbalization, and the adequacy of the constraint satisfaction achieved fosters a revision in the examinee's supraordinate working model of the test situation. Each card presentation confronts the examinee with a new opportunity for encoding, activation, and control, all in a dialectical interaction with working models of the evolving examiner-examinee relationship. In effect, the whole test process may be thought of a continuous shimmering state with more or less visible elements.

Once the "association" phase of the test is completed, a new set of constraints are imposed, namely the "inquiry" phase. The inquiry, a task of considerably less ambiguity than that provoked during the "what if" stage of the test, demands a justification about the verbalization in terms of the location and stimulus qualities of the blot. The "where is it?" and "what makes it look that way?" rule shift, provokes a significant change in the overall test schema. Here again the sorting of schemas occurs, along with the further opportunity to observe control processes, but within a narrower range of constraints than in the association phase.

Schema theory makes a significant further contribution to the interpretive process. Similar to other text based analysis for the elucidation of "role relationship models" or "core conflictual relationship themes" (Horowitz, 1991; Luborsky, Crits-Christoph, Friedman, Mark, & Schaffler, 1991), the test interpreter looks for material representing implicit or explicit self or self/other representations, with special weight given to those that are repeated, in order to derive inferences.

These applications of contemporary cognitive science models to Rorschach psychology demonstrate the vitality of the test in reflecting changing paradigms in general psychology. The advent of cognitive science models places the Rorschach into the "cognitive revolution" that has been going on now for almost two decades and sets the stage for considerations of the test from the perspectives of neuroscience and neuropsychology. The application of a cognitive science paradigm to the Rorschach provides new conceptual tools for understanding the test and generating hypotheses for research. As yet, no neuropsychological account of the Rorschach response process has been proposed, although the task requires a number of neuropsychological functions, including visual scanning and encoding, central processing and retrieval from long and short-term verbal and visual memory stores, patterns of sequential and holistic processing, cross channel translation from visual to linguistic modes (Gold, 1987), and verbalization. The Rorschach response process has yet to be examined from the perspective of real-time imaging techniques, such as PET scanning, a further opportunity to evaluate cerebral functions in light of the phases of the response process. Finally, the current contribution of cognitive science models has focused on the response process. Information processing approaches may be of great value in integrating data from the structural summary and their underlying processes into a theoretically coherent interpretive schema.

Acknowledgement

Thanks to Mardi J. Horowitz, M.D., Charles Stinson, M.D., and Charles A. Peterson, Ph.D. for their inspiration, to Evelynne Raposo for bibliographic assistance, and to Justin Phoenix Acklin for assistance with figures.

Résumé

Le Rorschach possède la remarquable capacité de refléter les paradigmes conceptuels dominants, et évolutifs, issus de la psychologie générale et de la psychologie clinique. Le présent article applique des instruments conceptuels récemment dégagés par les sciences cognitives au test du Rorschach, et tout particulièrement au processus de la réponse. L'intérêt d'appliquer des approches conceptuelles nouvelles au test est de mettre sous de nouvelles perspectives des phénomènes cliniques qui ont pu s'obscurcir par excès de familiarité ou en raison de la faiblesse du paradigme, d'élargir le débat sur ces phénomènes, et enfin de générer des hypothèses pertinentes pour la recherche empirique. La révolution cognitive en psychologie, qui connaît un développement parallèle dans les neurosciences et les sciences cognitives, a entraîné une révolution des modèles de traitement de l'information dans les processus cognitifs. Initialement modélisés d'après l'ordinateur digital, les modèles actuels considèrent les processus mentaux en termes similaires aux réseaux neuronaux, une métaphore de la cognition qui emprunte plus au cerveau qu'à l'ordinateur. Les modèles de réseaux neuronaux ou connexionnistes rendent mieux compte de la cognition réelle. Ces modèles sont fondés sur les hypothèses de représentation distribuée et du traitement parallèle distribué.

Une autre tendance dérivée de la psychologie cognitive est de considérer les processus mentaux en tant que "schèmes." La théorie des schèmes procure des instruments conceptuels efficaces pour comprendre les processus mentaux, qui comprennent l'encodage, l'interprétation et le traitement de l'expérience. Ces modèles sont appliqués au processus de la réponse Rorschach. Celuici est compris comme le résultat d'un traitement en distribution parallèle dans lequel de multiples schémas sont activés et manipulés par des processus défensifs de contrôle qui visent à satisfaire le maximum de contraintes. Cette façon de voir le processus de la réponse au Rorschach rend justice à la complexité et à la subtilité de la pensée de l'homme et permet de dépasser les conceptions en terme de "boîte noire." Les modèles des neurosciences et de la neuropsychologie représentent le fer de lance et la nouvelle vague de la conceptualisation des processus activés par et intriqués dans le Test du Rorschach.

Resumen

El Rorschach evidencia una notable capacidad para reflejar los paradigmas conceptuales dominantes—aunque en proceso de desarrollo—derivados de la psicología general y clínica. La presente contribución aplica al Rorschach—especificamente al proceso de respuesta—instrumentos conceptuales emergentes derivados de la ciencia cognitiva. El valor de aplicar nuevos enforques conceptuales al test consiste end que éstos permiten reconsiderar fenómenos clínicos que podrían haber sido obscurecidos por la familiaridad of debilidad del paradigma, así como extender el debate acerca de los fenómenos y generar, finalmente, hipótesis adecuadas para la investigación empírica. La revolución cognitiva en Psicología, con desarrollos paralelos en cognición y neurociencia, ha estimulado una revolución en los modelos de procesamiento de información de los procesos cognitivos. Modelados inicialmente en el computador digital, los modelos contemporáneos ven los procesos mentales en términos similares a las redes neuronales, al tomar al cerebro—y no a la computadora—como metáfora de la cognición. La red neuronal o los modelos conexionistas dan mejor cuenta de la cognición actual. Estos modelos están basados en postulados de representación distribuída y procesamiento paralelo distribuído.

Una segunda tendencia, derivada de la psicología cognitiva, consiste en la comprensión de los procesos mentales como "esquemas." La teoría de los esquemas provee instrumentos conceptuales útiles para entender los procesos mentales, incluyendo la codificación, interpretación y procesamiento d la experiencia. Estos modelos son aplicados al proceso de respuesta al Rorschach. Considerar al proceso de respuesta como el resultado de un procesamiento de distribución paralela—en el cual múltiples esquemas son activados y manipulados por procesos defensivos de control con las metas de restringir al máximo la satisfacción—hace justicia a la complejidad y sutileza del pensamiento humano y supera las perspectivas del tipo "caja negra" en cuanto al proceso de respuesta al Rorschach. La neurociencia y los modelos neuropsicológicos representan la orientación más novedosa, en cuanto a cómo conceptualizar los procesos activados por la prueba de Rorschach.

References

Acklin, M. W. (1991). Alexithymia, somatization, and the Rorschach response process. *Rorschachiana XVII*. Bern: Verlag Hans Huber.

Bartlett, F. C. (1932). *Remembering: A study in experimental and social psychology*. Cambridge: Cambridge University Press.

Baldwin, M. W. (1992). Relational schemas and the processing of social information. *Psychological Bulletin, 112*, 461–484.

Berger, D. (1954). Examiner influence on the Rorschach. *Journal of Clinical Psychology, 10*, 245–249.

Caspar, F., Rothenfluh, T., & Segal, Z. (1992). The appeal of connectionism for clinical psychology. *Clinical Psychology Review, 12*, 719–762.

Colligan S. C., & Exner, J. E. (1985). Responses of schizophrenics and nonpatients to a tachistoscopic presentation of the Rorschach. *Journal of Personality Assessment, 49*, 129–136.

Colligan S. C., & Exner, J. E. (1985). Responses of nonpatients to a one second tachistoscopic exposure of the Rorschach blots [Workshop Study No. 299, unpublished]. Rorschach Workshops, Asheville, NC.

Emde, R. (1988a). Developmental terminable and interminable: I. Innate and motivational factors from infancy. *International Journal of Psychoanalysis, 69*, 23–42.

Emde, R. (1988b). Development terminable and interminable: II. Recent psychoanalytic theory and considerations. *International Journal of Psychoanalysis, 69*, 283–296.

Erdberg, P. (1993). The U.S. Rorschach scene: Integration and elaboration. In I. Weiner (Ed.). *Rorschachiana XVII: Yearbook of the International Rorschach Society*. Seattle: Hogrefe & Huber Publishers.

Exner, J. E. (1986a). *The Rorschach: A comprehensive system. Volume 1: Basic Foundations* (2nd ed). New York: Wiley.

Exner, J. E. (1986 b). Searching for projection in the Rorschach. *Journal for Personality Assessment, 53, 520–536.*

Exner, J. E. (1991). *The Rorschach: A comprehensive system. Volume 2: Interpretation* (2nd ed.). New York: Wiley.

Feldman, J., & Ballard, D. H. (1982). Connectionist models and their properties. *Cognitive Science, 6,* 205–254.

Fodor, J. A., & Pylyshyn, Z. (1988). Connectionism and cognitive architecture: A critical analysis. *Cognition, 28,* 3–71.

Gibby, R. G. (1952). Examiner influence on Rorschach inquiry. *Journal of Consulting Psychology, 16,* 449–455.

Gold, J. (1987). The role of verbalization in the Rorschach response process: A review. *Journal of Personality Assessment, 51,* 489–505.

Greenberg, R., & Gordon, M. (1983). Examiner's sex and children's Rorschach productivity. *Psychological Reports, 53,* 355–357.

Greenwald, A. G. (1992). New look 3: Unconscious cognition reclaimed. *American Psychologist, 47,* 766–779.

Horowitz, M. J. (1987). *States of mind: Configurational analysis of individual psychology. 2nd edition.* New York: Plenum.

Horowitz, M. J. (1988). *Introduction to psychodynamics: A new synthesis.* New York: Basic Books.

Horowitz, M. J. (1989). Relationship schema formulation: Role-relationship models and intrapsychic conflict. *Psychiatry, 52,* 260–274.

Horowitz, M. J. (1991). *Person schemas and maladaptive interpersonal patterns.* Chicago: University of Chicago Press.

Horowitz, M. J. (1991 b). States, schemas, and control: General theories for psychotherapy integration. *Journal of Psychotherapy Integration, 1,* 85–102.

Horowitz, M. J., Fridhandler, B., & Stinson, C. (1991). Person schemas and emotion. *Journal of the American Psychoanalytic Association, 39,* 173–208.

Horowitz, M., Cooper, S., Fridhandler, B., Bond, M., & Vaillant, G. (1992). Control processes and defense mechanisms. *Journal of Psychotherapy Research and Practice, 1,* 324–336.

Ingram, R., & Kendall, P. (1986). Cognitive clinical psychology: Implications of an information processing perspective. In R. E. Ingram (Ed.). *Information processing approaches to clinical psychology.* New York: Academic Press.

Luborsky, L., Crits-Christoph, P., Friedman, S., Mark, D., & Schaffler, P. (1991). Freud's transference template compared with the core conflictual relationship theme (CCRT): Illustrations by the two specimen cases. In M. J. Horowitz (ed.), *Persons schemas and maladaptive inpersonal patterns.* Chicago: University of Chicago Press.

Kosslyn, S. M., & Koenig, O. (1992). *Wet mind: The new cognitive science.* New York: Free Press.

McClelland, J. L., Rumelhart, D. E., & Hinton, G. E. (1986). The appeal of parallel distributed processing. In J. L. McClelland and the PDP research group (Eds.).

Parallel distributed processing: Explorations in the microstructure of cognition. Volume 1: Foundations. Cambridge: MIT Press.

Norman, D. A. (1986). Reflections on cognition and parallel distributing processing. In J. McClelland, D. Rumelhart and the PDP Research Group (Eds.). *Parallel distributed processing: Explorations in the microstructure of cognition. Volume 2: Psychological and biological models.* Cambridge: MIT Press.

Palmer, S. E., Kimchi, R. (1986). The information processing approach to cognition. In J. Knapp & Lynn Robertson (Eds.). *Approaches to cognition: Contrast and controversies.* Hillsdale, NJ: LEA Associates.

Peterson, C. A., & Schilling, K. (1983). Card pull in projective testing. *Journal of Personality Assessment, 47,* 265–275.

Phillips, L., & Smith, J. (1954). *Rorschach interpretation: Advanced interpretation.* New York: Grune & Stratton.

Rapaport, D., Gill, M., & Schafer, R. (1968). *Diagnostic psychological testing.* New York: International Universities Press.

Rorschach, H. (1969). *Psychodiagnostics.* New York: Grune & Stratton.

Rosenblatt, F. (1962). *Principles of neurodynamics.* New York: Spartan.

Rumelhart, D., Smolensky, P., McClelland, J., & Hinton, G. (1986). Schemata and sequential thought processes in PDP models. In J. McClelland, D. Rumelhart and the PDP Research Group (Eds.). *Parallel Distributed Processing. Explorations in the microstructure of cognition. Volume 2: Psychological and biological models.* Cambridge: MIT Press.

Schachtel, E. (1966). *Experiential foundations of Rorschach's test.* London: Tavistock Publications.

Schafer, R. (1954). *Psychoanalytic interpretation in Rorschach testing.* New York: Grune & Stratton.

Smith, B. L. (1990). Potential space and the Rorschach: An application of object relations theory. *Journal of Personality Assessment, 55,* 756–767.

Stein, D. (1992). Clinical cognitive science: Possibilities and limitations. In D. J. Stein & J. E. Young (Eds.). *Cognitive science and clinical disorders.* New York: Academic Press.

Stein, D., & Young, J. E. (1992). *Cognitive science and clinical disorders.* New York: Academic Press.

Stern, D. (1985). *The interpersonal world of the infant: A view from psychoanalysis and developmental psychology.* New York: Basic Books.

Stinson, C., & Palmer, S. (1991). Parallel distributed processing models of person schemas and psychopathologies. In M. J. Horowitz (Ed.). *Person schemas and maladaptive interpersonal patterns.* Chicago: University of Chicago Press.

Rorschach's Psychodiagnosis in Peru

Matilde Raez de Ramirez

Pontifical Catholic University of Peru

Peru, as a multilingual and multicultural country, with differing and sometimes even antagonistic values and modes of conduct, poses a challenge to psychologists in relation to the instruments and techniques that they use. Rorschach psychodiagnosis, because of the breadth and variety of the information that it reveals, makes it possible to study the structure and contents of normal personality and also to diagnose psychopathology. Above all in its importance for our country, being an unstructured instrument in which the instructions have little influence, it can be applied to different groups independently of their culture, sex, or age.

The present article consists of a brief historical review of the Rorschach method in Peru since its introduction. We identify the areas of work in which it has been utilized as well as the approaches most often used, the research studies that have been conducted, and perspectives for the future.

Research, the basis of scientific knowledge, constitutes the central point of our presentation, because it indicates the development of the technique and its present status in all fields of psychological endeavor, including clinical, educational, social, industrial, and forensic psychology, and its place in prevention, diagnosis, treatment, and teaching. It is not possible to recount the development of a technique without relating it to the investigative efforts that allow for its evaluation and improvement.

Antecedents of the Rorschach in Peru

Rorschach psychodiagnosis first came to our country in 1920, when Hermann Rorschach sent the cards and text of his test to Professor Honorio Delgado, a prominent Peruvian psychiatrist who was one of the best known psychiatrists in Latin America at that time. After receiving the material through Dr. Fernando Allende, a Chilean psychiatrist, Professor Delgado became interested in the technique and began immediately to employ it and to acquaint colleagues with it.

These developments led in October of 1924 to the appearance of the first article about Rorschach's work in the Peruvian medical literature. Entitled "The Application of the Form Interpretation Test," it was a posthumous work of Rorschach published by Emil Oberholzer. The publication of this article gave proof to the dedication of Dr. Honorio Delgado to promoting familiarity with the test in Peru. It was Delgado, moreover, who was first to introduce the technique into clinical diagnostic work in the forensic field, when in 1927 he applied the test in a blind diagnostic study of a delinquent youth.

The Rorschach Between 1924 and 1965

During this time the test was used primarily by psychiatrists. Psychology as a career was initiated in the 1950s at the National University of San Marcos (a public institution) and in 1958 at the Pontifical Catholic University (a private institution). At this stage of its development in Peru, the Rorschach was used individually in clinical and forensic evaluations and also in numerous group studies in small communities, frequently with difficulty in generalizing from the results.

It is important to mention the following researchers for their valuable contributions and their strong interest in the method. Dr. Esteban Hidalgo (1938) applied it to 180 children ages 10 to 12 living in an orphanage and presented his results at the first meeting of the Panamerican Neuropsychiatric Society in Santiago, Chile.

Luis A. Guerra, an eminent professor at the University of San Marcos, began in 1946 to use the Rorschach in clinical work with children and completed numerous studies of experiential types and their frequency in this country.

Federico Sal y Rosas (1950) worked particularly on location choice and its value in diagnosis.

Beginning in 1951, Dr. Jose Sanchez Garcia introduced Klopfer's approach, and later, in 1958, he became actively involved in research as a professor at the Pontifical Catholic University.

Dr. Sanchez Garcia conducted the first transcultural study in 1951, with a group of Aguanuras (a jungle tribe), and demonstrated with his work the value of the Rorschach and its application in different communities independently of their cultural level of development. Another interesting contribution in 1951 was "Rorschach Study of the Problem of Form in 850 Adult Subjects with Different Levels of Education," which Garcia used as his baccalaureate thesis in Lima at the San Marcos University.

In 1959 there was "Rorschach Psychodiagnosis in Some Prisons in Lima," published in the *Journal of the Police Health Department.*

Pedro Aliaga Lindo (1954), with "Comparative Study of Rorschach's Test in 238 Children in Huachoc [an Indian community] and in Lima," continued the transcultural line of research to obtain his baccalaureate in medicine at the University of San Marcos. In Quito, Ecuador, in 1962, Lindo presented a valuable contribution on "The Vicissitudes of Rorschach's Test in Peru," which was published as an issue of *Criminology, Neuropsychiatry, and Related Disciplines.*

The first contributions of psychologists to the Rorschach literature in Peru began to appear in the 1960s, with such outstanding papers as one by Luis Estrada de los Rios in 1962 on "The Rorschach in Murderers," which was his baccalaureate thesis in psychology at the University of San Marcos.

The Rorschach Between 1965 and 1980

In this period the Rorschach continued to be used mainly in the clinical and forensic areas for personality diagnosis and in the educational area for comparative study of groups from different socioeconomic backgrounds. During this time it became a basic tool of psychologists and was no longer used by psychiatrists. This development was due to the fact that the technique was being taught in universities by and for psychologists but was not being taught in any medical school.

Most of the research studies conducted were theses for obtaining the baccalaureate degree in psychology, which in Peru is earned by presenting a piece of investigative work. Another way in which the Rorschach was used involved case studies, which also served an important function. In Peru obtaining the title of Licensed Psychologist requires presentation and defense of a case study.

Table 1. Investigations done with Rorschach in Peru, 1924–1965.

Areas	No.	%
Clinical	28	75.6
Transcultural	4	10.8
Social	3	8.3
Educational	1	2.7
Test's history	1	2.7
Total	37	100.0

The fact that most of the research studies were done in university settings was due to the limited investigative possibilities in other contexts, in which financial support for research was seldom available.

The clinical area continued to be the one with the majority of published works (77.1%), covering a broad range of topics. Most of these investigations centered on groups with psychosomatic disorders, together with diagnostic categories and addictions.

During this time multidisciplinary investigations also started taking place. Alfredo Ramirez, an endocrinologist, and Matilde Raez, a psychologist, described a case of true hermaphroditism (1970) in which the Rorschach data determined the biological sex change, based primarily on indications of the patient's gender identification. With respect to use of the technique as a prognostic indicator, the work of Gustavo Delgado Aparicio (1974) is also important to mention; this work concerned Rorschach indicators of ego strength in drug addicts.

In the field of forensic psychology, the test was used in supporting expert testimony in legal cases. It proved particularly helpful in evaluating young people in cases involving issues of adoption, special schooling, and residential placement. It also found application in the work of the Military Justice Administration, the Second Juridical Police Zone, and the staff of the Police Hospital.

Beginning in 1974 the Consensus Rorschach was introduced for the study of couples, families, and small groups. Max Hernandez, who had been working in the Tavistock Clinic in London, brought the material to Peru, and Matilde Raez systematized it. Its use in the clinic makes it possible to work simultaneously with people individually and with couples or families as a whole. The similarities and differences between data obtained from individuals and their family groups facilitates therapeutic work and preventive intervention with groups.

The Rorschach Between 1981 and 1993

In the last decade Peru has passed through a time of particular crisis due to phenomena of violence, vandalism, terrorism, and drug traffic never before found in our country. The need to understand these phenomena has required of psychology work with groups and more creative and rigorous use of our techniques. What has been emphasized is the psychosocial aspect of this field of study and the necessity of going beyond the study of the individual to deal with large segments of the population to explore complex psychological phenomena without losing sight of qualitative individual aspects of personality functioning.

The investigation of social variables has increased by 23.6%, while studies with the Rorschach have decreased in the educational field, which has utilized other techniques. Subjects such as violence, empathy, identity, affect, and ego strength have appeared that reflect conflicts and also the search for resources that will enable elaboration of these conflicts.

The presence of research groups in universities has become noteworthy. In the San Martin de Porras University, young psychologists such as Jesus Romero Croce and Pedro Jaramillo have specialized in the clinical field.

In the Catholic University a group of teachers formed by Matilde Raez, Patricia Martinez, Isabel Nino de Guzman, and Zoila Rossell (1985, 1986) on the basis of their all having clinical and research experience, decided to use a group form of the Rorschach in order to apply the test to a larger number of people without sacrificing the most valuable elements of projection. The technique consists of presenting slides of the Rorschach cards, to which groups of subjects are asked to write their spontaneous responses. The responses are scored according to the codes

Table 2. Investigations done with Rorschach in Peru, 1966–1980.

Areas	No.	%
Clinical	27	77.1
Transcultural	1	2.8
Social	3	8.5
Educational	2	5.7
Organizational	2	5.7
Total	35	100.0

of Klopfer and of Raez and her collaborators, consisting of 115 variables grouped in interpretive categories that correspond to operationalized theoretical concepts.

In 1989 this group just mentioned earned for the first time a Social Sciences research award. Their subject, "Study of Identity Formation in Women Organized According to Marginal Urban Sectors," provided affirmation of usefulness of the technique in examining this phenomenon. A book based on this research is presently in press.

Dora Frisancho (1989) from the San Marcos University added to this research area with a study "Contribution to the Elaboration of an Andean Rorschach Profile."

Investigations with the Rorschach involving suicidal individuals, criminal offenders sentenced to death, and terrorists have enabled psychologists to question the real nature of these phenomena and to contribute valuable information from the psychological point of view concerning prevention in cases of suicide risk, improved intervention with the populace in cases of terrorism, and the usefulness of the death penalty, which some are trying to reintroduce. These developments account for the fact that the Rorschach has become a valuable tool for psychologists seeking to serve as agents of social change.

Future Perspectives

What is the present situation of the Rorschach in Peru? In the field of psychology, it is being taught in almost every university that offers this specialty (77.7%), with Klopfer's approach being the most widely used. Within psychology, the Rorschach occupies a particularly important position among psychological tests. As an example, the 1991 National

Table 3. Investigations done with Rorschach in Peru, 1981–1993.

Areas	No.	%
Clinical	26	68.4
Social	9	23.6
Clinical & Social	1	2.6
Transcultural	1	2.6
Technical	1	2.6
Total	35	100.0

Congress of Psychology included an invited lecture on the use of the Rorschach and two special courses on the method: one by Luis Estrada from the San Marcos University on "Systems of Rorschach Psychodiagnosis" and one by Matilde Raez from the Pontificial Catholic University on "Recent Advances in Rorschach Psychodiagnosis."

Our goals are to perfect the application of the Rorschach technique in groups, to unify the coding system, to deepen the fields of research, and to participate more actively in the international scientific community.

Résumé

Le travail présenté constitue un aperçu historique du développement et de l'utilisation du Rorschach au Pérou. La méthode Rorschach a été introduite au Pérou dans les années 20 par Honorio Delgado, psychiatre de renom, et elle fut utilisé et tudiée principalement par des psychiatres pendant de nombreuses années. La psychologie ne devint un cursus professionnel dans les universités péruviennes que dans les années 50, et c'est à cette époque que les psychologues commencèrent à s'approprier la technique. De nos jours, la méthode Rorschach est enseignée au sein du cursus de psychologie dans la plupart des universités qui dispensent des diplômes en psychologie. Elle n'est plus du tout enseignée dans les facultés de médecine.

Dans les premières années, et jusqu'en 1965, le Rorschach était utilisé en clinique infantile comme en clinique adulte et il entra dans le champ de la psychologie légale. A partir de 1951, de nombreuses études transculturelles ont été produites, portant sur des sujets issus de diverses communautés minoritaires, de divers milieux socioéconomiques, ainsi que de divers contextes culturels y compris des tribus de la jungle. La nature peu structurée du Rorschach et l'impact négligeable de sa consigne en ont permis une utilisation large dans un pays aussi multiculturel que le Pérou.

La méthode la plus employée au Pérou a été celle de Klopfer, mais le consensus Rorschach a aussi reçu une attention considérable parmi les psychologues qui travaillent avec des couples et des familles. Depuis une dizaine d'années, et en raison des turbulences sociales et politiques, la recherche est passée de l'évaluation individuelle à des analyses des influences de groupes qui conduisent à des phénomènes tels que la violence, le vandalisme, le terrorisme et le trafic de drogue. De nombreux psychologues se préoccupent de trouver comment les résultats Rorschach pourraient les aider produire des changements sociaux. A cet égard, Raez et ses collègues se sont intéressés aux méthodes d'administration en groupe afin de pouvoir appliquer la technique à de plus nombreuses personnes.

Au Pérou, nos objectifs sont de nous perfectionner dans la technique du Rorschach, d'intensifier nos efforts de recherche, et de nous investir plus activement dans la communauté scientifique internationale.

Resumen

Este trabajo presenta un breve resumen histórico del desarrollo y utilización del Rorschach en el Perú. El método Rorschach fué introducido en el país en la década de los veinte pro el eminente psiquiatra Honorio Delgado, siendo usado y estudiado predominantemente por psiquiatras durante en largo periodo. Fué apenas a partir de los años cincuenta que la Psicología se introdujo como carrera en las universidades peruanas, con lo cual los psicólogos comenzaron a reemplazar a los psiquiatras en el trabajo con la técnica. Actualmente el método Rorschach es enseñado dentro del programa conducente al titulo de Psicólogo en la mayoría de las universidades, no formando parte del pensum de estudios de ninguna Escuela de Medicina.

Ya antes de 1965, el Rorschach era aplicado clínicamente tanto a niños como a adultos y se le utilizaba en evaluaciones forenses. A partier de 1951 se vienen realizando numerosos estudios transculterales con el Rorschach, en los cuales se utilizan sujectos deo pequeñas comunidades de my distinto tipo, asi como de variadas circunstancias socioeconómicas y desarrollo cultural, incluyendo tribus de la jungla. La naturaleza inestructurada del Rorschach y la sencillez de su consigna hacen de él un instrumento muy conviente para ser aplicade en un país tan diverso culturalmente como lo es el Perú.

El enfoque de Klopfer ha sido el más ampliamente utilizado en el país; por otra parte, el Rorschach Consensual ha recibido considerable atención pro parte de psicólogos que trabajan con parejas y familias. En la última década, coincidiendo con la emergencia de una gran agitación social y política en el Perú, los intereses de los investigadores se han desplazado de la evaluación individual al análisis de las influencias de grupo que conducen a fenómenos tales como la violencia, el vandalismo, el terrorismo y el tráfico de drogas. Muchos psicólogos están buscando la manera de utilizar los hallazgos del Rorscach en sus esfuerzos para constituirse en agentes efectivos del cambio social. A este respecto, Raez y sus colegas vienen prestado particular atención a los métodos de administración colectiva con el objeto de aplicar el Rorschach a grupos mayores de sujectos.

Los objectivos que nos proponemos alcanzar en este momento son: perfeccionar la aplicación de la técnica, expandir nuestros esfuerzos de investigación e involucrarnos más activamente en la comunidad cientifica internacional.

References

Aliaga, P. (1962). *La prueba de Rorschach en el Perú*. Separata de criminología, Neuro-Psiquiatría y Disciplinas Conexas. 'Lima.

Aliaga, P. (1954). *Estudio comparativo de la prueba de Rorschach in 238 ninos de Huachac (pueblo indigina y serrano) y Lima*. Lima: U.N.M.S.M.

Delgado, G. (1974). *La incidencia de la droga en el debilitamiento del ego según algunos indicadores de Rorschach*. Lima: U.R.P.

Estrada, L. (1962). *Rorschach en Homicidas*. Tesis para optar el grado de bachiller in psicologia. Lima: U.N.M.S.M.

Frisancho, D. (1989). *Contribución a la elaboración de un perfil Rorschach Andino*. Lima: U.N.M.S.M.

Guerra, L. y Pisculich, E. (1946). *Aplicación de la prueba de Rorschach a 114 menores tutelados con el objeto de estudiar los tipos de vivencias*. Revista Penal y de tutela, Volumen V año III. Lima.

Hidalgo, E. (1938). *Aplicación de la prueba de Rorschach a 180 niños de 10 a 12 años de edad, asilados en el hogar infantil*. Chile: Primera reunión de las jornadas Neuro-Psiquiátricas Panamericanas (781-782).

Nino de Guzman, M. (1984). *Aspectos de la afectividad del obeso a través del Psicodiagnóstico de Rorschach*. Lima: P.U.C.

Raez, M. y Martinez, P. (1985). *Una approximacion a la violencia a través de contenidos de Rorschach en personal encargado de un centro de adaptación*. Lima: Revista de Psicología, P.U.C. año III, Vol. III, No. 2.

Ráez, M.; Rossel, Z.; NiÑo de guzmán, I; Martínez, P.; Figueroa, M. (1986) *El Psicodiagnóstico de Rorschach como instrumento evaluador de grupos, un estudio de 1200 casos*. Lima: Revista de Psicología, P.U.C. Año IV, Vol. IV, No. 1.

Ráez, M. Martínez, P., Niño de Guzmán, I., Rossell Z. y Figueroa, M. (1986). *Situación del anciano en el Perú. Z. Gerontol* 19: 118-121.

Ráez, M. Martínez, P. Niño de Guzmán, I. y Rossell, Z. (1993). *Estudio evolutivo de identidad en mujeres organizadas de sectores urbano-marginales.* Libro en prensa, Lima.

Ramírez, a. y Ráez, M. (1970). *Simposium: Intersexualidad a propósito de un caso de Hermafroditismo Verdadero.* Lima: Revista de la sanidad de las Fuerzas Policiales, Vol. 31: 43–57.

Rossell, Z. (1987. *Approximacion al psicodiagnostice de Rorschach infantil.* Lima P.U.C. año V, Vol. V, No. 1.

Sánchez-García, J. (1951). *El Rorschach para estudiar el problema de la forma en 850 sujetos adultos de diversos grados de instrucción (primaria), secundaria, universitaria).* Lima: tesis para optar el Bachillerato, U.N.M.S.M.

Sánchez-Garcia, J. (1953). *El Rorschach en los Aguarunas.* Madrid: Revista general de Psicología aplicada, vol. 14.

Sánchez-García, J. (1958). *Los Indios Aguarunas vistos a través del Rorschach.* Lima: Boletín del Departamento de Higiene Mental, Nos. 4–5.

Sal y Rosas, F: Jerí, R. y Sánchez, J. (1950). *El Psicodiagnóstico de Rorschach para estudiar la localización de las respuestas con sistemas de localizadores propios.* Lima: Rev. Neuro-Psiquiatría, tomo XII, No. 4.

Recurring Objects in Rorschach Records over a Period of about 30 Years: How Often Do People Report the Same Thing Again?

Harald Janson and Håkan Stattin

Department of Psychology, Stockholm University, Sweden

The issue of the temporal stability of Rorschach responses has been addressed frequently (e. g., Exner, 1980; Exner, Armbruster, & Viglione, 1978). Studies employed to develop of the Comprehensive System (Exner, 1986; 1991) have generally shown high temporal stability over periods up to three years for most variables included in the System. Many issues of stability or development in the Rorschach may well be addressed through the use of longitudinal data. However, there are few studies in which a group of subjects has been followed over a considerable period of time and tested repeatedly.

At the Stockholm Laboratory for Longitudinal Research on Individual Development we have access to Rorschach data for a group of 212 subjects, covering a period of about 30 years. In a first attempt to find meaningful ways of describing temporal stability in this material, we focused on the stability of localization and content in the records of a small subsample. Our interest was awakened by the many spontaneous comments made by members of our study group in the course of administration of the Rorschach at 35 years of age that they remembered what they had seen in the blots on earlier occasions. After making such a comment, some subjects went on to repeat, more or less verbatim, all their responses to the same blot 17 years previously; others, however, delivered a response that had not been recorded on any of eight earlier test occasions. Our point of departure consisted in posing the simple question, "How often do people report the same object again?" We were interested both in obtaining an overall frequency for the recurrence of objects over the years and in establishing whether objects located in different types of blot areas, or objects with different Form Quality, Popular, or Content codings, recurred with the same or different frequencies. Further, we wished to see whether there was a difference in rates of recurrence between groups of subjects whose lives had differed in a certain respect. Our tentative hypothesis was that stability in Rorschach records would be related to stability in interpersonal relations. A history of relatively stable, and less unhappy, relationships in the life of a person was hypothesized to entail greater access to feelings and memories, which would be reflected in greater stability of Rorschach reponses. To examine this hypthesis, two extreme groups of subjects (the one with stable, the other with unstable relationship histories) were selected and compared with regard to temporal stability.

Method

Subjects

The data come from the Solna study, a Swedish birth-to-maturity study (Karlberg, Klackenberg, Engström, Klackenberg-Larsson, Lichtenstein, Stensson, & Svennberg, 1968). The original study group comprised a sample of 212 subjects in an urban community, 122 males and 90 females; these subjects have been studied prospectively from birth up to the present time (the age of 35 to 38). They were born between the years 1955 and 1958, being the offspring of women visiting the Solna Antenatal Clinic over a three-year period. Every fourth mother was asked to participate in a long-term study of the development of their children. Of these mothers only 3% refused the invitation to participate. A pilot group of 29 subjects was added. Comparisons on relevant variables have shown the group of subjects to be representative of Swedish urban communities (Karlberg et al, 1968). Data on pediatric, psychological, psychiatric and social factors of various kinds were collected annually, from an early age (of the subjects) up to and including the age of 18. Subsequent data collections took place when the subjects were in adulthood, at the ages of around 21, 25 and 35.

For the present study, twenty persons were selected from the total study group: ten males and ten females, half with a background of stable relationships, and half with a life-experience of unstable relationships.

Members of the "stable" group had lived in intact families up to the age of 18; annual maternal reports showed a good relationship between

157

father and mother during upbringing; and, on the latest occasion of follow-up, they had been married to, or cohabiting with, the same person for at least 12 years.

Members of the "unstable" group had experienced parental divorce or a change in one provider of care or the loss of one parent before the age of 18; their mothers had reported problematic spousal relations on at least 3 of the annual occasions of investigation; and, on the latest occasion of follow-up, they were either not cohabiting or had been cohabiting for no longer than 7 years.

It was further decided to exclude any subject with missing records at the ages of 4 or 35, and any with more than three missing records at other ages. However, for none of the selected subjects three records were actually missing; just one had two, while five subjects had one.

Data

The Rorschach had been administered to all subjects in the original study group on nine occasions: at the ages of 4, 5, 6, 7, 8, 10, 14, and 18; and, on follow-up, when they were around 35 years of age. The Klopfer-Beck system was used for administration and scoring. Up to the age of 18, with few exceptions, testing was carried out within a period of 14 days before or after the subject's birthday. On each occasion the participation rate was 80% or higher of living subjects. On some occasions, up to the age of 18, and for the majority of subjects at the latest follow-up, testing was performed by a psychologist with brief training in the administration of the Rorschach.

Coding

To consider the issue addressed in the simplest and most straightforward manner, we analyzed the records by reported objects, not by responses. (A response can contain several objects, each of which may or may not have been reported on earlier occasions.) However, not all percepts or contents in the responses could easily be coded as separate objects. To treat part of a response as an object, three criteria had to be met: the object had to be located in a distinct blot area; the object had to be distinguishable from other objects in the same response; and further, the division of the response into objects should not alter the coding of other objects in a way that would violate descriptions of the latter. (Thus, for example, blood and items of clothing were often *not* coded as separate objects.)

For each subject all the different objects reported on any occasion were tabulated separately for each Card. For each object, a record was kept of Location, Form Quality, Popular and Content codings, and at what age, or ages, of the subject it had been reported. The concept of "first occurrence" is used below to refer to the first report of an object in the history of a subject, and that of "recurrence" to any subsequent reports of the same object.

The different codings followed the working tables for the Comprehensive System (Exner, 1990), although some adaptations were made in the light of the specific purposes of the study. The Form Quality and Popular codings were combined into one variable, with the categories Popular, Ordinary, Unusual and Minus. All objects were assigned a Form Quality coding, even objects that ordinarily would have been coded *No Form*. No object was assigned a Form Quality level of +. When an object had more than one content,the secondary content was also coded (e. g., as H,Cg for a person with an item of clothing). Occasionally, the primary content was not unequivocally codable (e. g., a part of the body might be *Hd* or *Ad*); in such cases, an alternative content code was noted. In the infrequent instances when two or more D areas were designated collectively in a somewhat arbitrary or vague manner (e. g., "All these look like birds" to the D15, D7 and D13 areas of Card X), the report was coded as a single object and assigned the Location code *Dd*.

Some scope was allowed for objects to be reported differently over the years and still be considered "the same." Generally, however, no change in primary Content coding or Form Quality coding was tolerated, and only minor variations in localization. When the localization of an object varied from one year to another, the alternative localization was noted in addition to the first.

It was not always an unambiguous decision to code an object as "the same as," or "different from," an earlier reported object; frequently, "calling" an object was a matter of judgment. The Working Tables for Form Quality in the Comprehensive System were used as a guideline; if two contents could be referred to one single table entry, we were inclined to code as "the same." There follow some examples of the variations that we regarded as tolerable:

– For the Popular D1 area of card VIII, animals of different species that met the requirements for the listing in the Tables, i. e., were "appropriate to contours," were considered "the same" object.

159

- "Plant" and "tree" in Card VIII were considered "the same," while localization was allowed to vary between W and D6.
- In Card VII, the localizations of D1, D2, and half of W were accepted for the Popular human figure.

However, the Popular responses of Bat or Butterfly to Cards I and V, and also the responses of Spider or Crab to the D1 area of Card X were always coded as different objects, since they are defined as different Popular responses in the Comprehensive System.

All codes for the present study were assigned by the first author (H.J.). About 5% of the material was also coded by a second psychologist, who had received three pages of written instructions and about two hours of training. An agreement of 84% was found for the division of the responses into objects and the coding of these objects as "the same" or "different." For comparable objects, the agreement was 91% for Localization, 83% for Form Quality, and 89% for primary Content coding.

Measure of recurrence

In order to compare the relative stabilities of different categories of objects, a crude statistical measure of recurrence was adopted. This involved dividing the number of recurrences in a class of objects by the number of first occurrences in that class. This measure is referred to below as the *rate of recurrence*. The theoretical maximum on this measure is 8.0 in the present material, which is the score of a category that reoccurs without exception; i. e., objects in that category are reported on all nine testing occasions, thus recurring eight times. Although the measure was found useful for comparing the relative recurrence rates of different classes of objects, it does not provide a basis for comparison with normative materials. Also it has certain specific disadvantages, e. g., that no account is taken of age at first occurrence.

Results

The total number of different objects over all subjects and Cards was 2092. Thus, the mean number of different objects reported per subject was 104.6. As can be seen from Figure 1, the number of reported objects per record varied with age of the subjects.

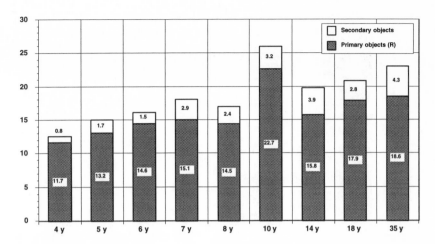

Figure 1. Mean number of reported primary objects (R) and secondary objects per record at different ages.

The number of objects per record increased slightly over the years. There was a temporary discontinuity in this trend at the age of 10, at which many more objects were reported than at any other age. This seems to be related to the high verbal and intellectual productivity that is associated with this age. It cannot completely be ruled out, however, that this discontinuity might be due in part to subtle changes in the test setting at this particular period in the investigation, that were not considered important at the time.

As it was noted, on each occasion, whether an object was the primary or secondary object of a response, the number of primary objects at each year approximately equals the number of responses in the records. This number is represented by the shaded part of the stacks. (The exception concerns those rare instances when the same object appeared twice in the same record.)

The mean rate of recurrence for all reported objects in the material was .53. The recurrence rate, however, varied greatly between different classes of responses. In Figure 2 are shown the rates of recurrence for objects with different Popular and Form Quality codings. As each object was assigned to only one category, no Popular objects are found in the other categories.

Popular and Ordinary objects recurred much more frequently than Unusual or Minus objects. By definition, P and o responses are those that occur frequently across records, and even by chance we can expect

161

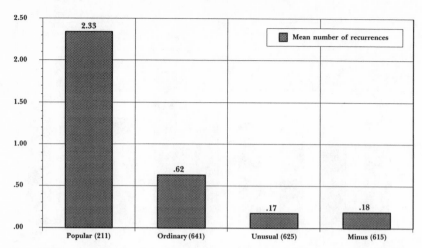

Figure 2. Recurrences per first occurrence by popular and form quality coding.

a high frequency of recurrence for objects in these categories. However, there is no a priori reason for responses that are rare in inter-individual comparisons to recur seldom within the same individual. But this, as can be seen from Figure 2, was found to be the case in our study: Unusual or Minus objects recurred significantly less often than Popular or Ordinary ones (p<.001, χ^2 = 645.55, DF = 3). Of all reported u or – objects, only about every sixth recurred, even on one occasion, in the history of a subject.

Minus responses may result from poor information processing or mediation, or may contain projection; for these reasons, it is possible to imagine that they will be less easily remembered. What is perhaps more remarkable is that Unusual objects recur with the same low rate as Minus responses.

Figure 3 shows the recurrence rates for objects in different types of blot areas. The 91 objects that differed slightly in location between years have been included in the "larger" of the two noted location categories. (For instance, if an object's location was coded as D on one occasion and Dd on another, that object has been assigned to the D category.)

As can be seen from Figure 3, the recurrence rate for objects located in Dd areas was considerably lower than for objects in other areas. This finding was statistically significant (p<.001; χ^2 = 114.14; DF = 2). Fewer than every twelfth Dd object recurred, even on one occasion, in the history of a subject. The Dd location code stands for different things: tiny details; combinations of D areas into a single object; arbitrary delimita-

162

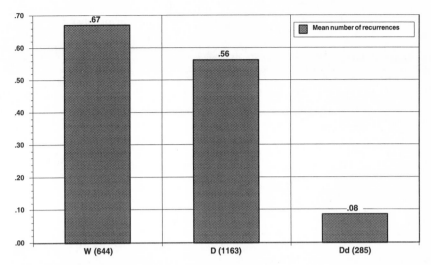

Figure 3. Recurrences per first occurrence by location.

tion of blot areas; and, in a few cases in the present study, a collective and somewhat arbitrary designation of two or more *D* areas. Some of these response patterns may represent less than satisfactory information processing. In other cases, they may indicate some kinds of defensive operations through which the subject avoids having to deal with other impressions from the blot. In both cases, it can be envisaged that responses will be less easily remembered.

The recurrence rate for objects that at one time or another included the use of Space was .44, as compared with .54 for objects that did not. This difference was not statistically significant. The relative recurrence rates for different contents varied considerably. Table 1 shows the mean number of recurrences per first occurrence by primary Content coding.

Whole Human Content had the highest rate of recurrence; it was the only Content category with an average of more than one recurrence per first occurence. It was followed by fictional or mythological Human Content and whole Animal Content, while most of the other frequently-recurring Contents were among the remaining Human and Animal categories. Relatively frequently-recurring categories were Clothing, Blood and Household, which often occur in conjunction with a living object.

It could be said that the objects that most often recurred were either living objects or items that are "on" or "together with" them. It would seem that these contents are more easily remembered. In those cases where objects are reported "together," the response being a synthesis of

Table 1. Mean number of recurrences per first occurrence by primary content coding.

Content Category	Mean No Occurrences	First Recurrences
H	1.47	109
(H)	0.86	66
A	0.77	713
Ad	0.49	195
Cg	0.47	60
Bl	0.37	19
Hd	0.37	90
Cl	0.35	37
(Hd)	0.33	27
Ls	0.32	95
Hh	0.31	81
Na	0.25	92
Bt	0.24	106
Ex	0.24	17
Fi	0.21	24
(A)	0.19	31
An	0.16	58
Art	0.15	54
Id	0.12	42
Fd	0.11	27
Sc	0.10	125

two or more objects, the subject will have put considerable energy into processing the stimulus, and it is reasonable to assume that he or she will more easily remember these objects. It must be borne in mind, however, that all of the Popular, and many possible Ordinary, responses to the blots are Human or Animal, so higher recurrence rates would be expected for these categories even by chance.

The recurrence rates of the Content categories included in the Isolate index formed a cluster at a rate of around .30, with the Cloud content as the most frequently recurring. Among the Content categories with the lowest rates of recurrence were Anatomy, Art, Food and Science. It is possible that these contents are less easily remembered because the underlying response processes in many cases include projection-like processes or defensive operations.

So far, we have simply presented summary data for the mean recurrence of objects across all years, and thus ignored the developmental aspect of stability. We shall now turn to this aspect.

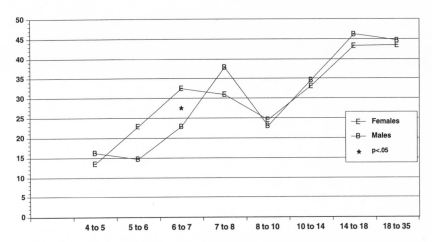

Figure 4. Year-to-year agreement of reported objects (%) for females and males.

In order to illustrate the year-to-year recurrence of objects, a measure of agreement between records adjacent in time was calculated separately for each interval, taking account only of the objects that appeared in the records on the actual two occasions. The percentages in Figure 4 represent the proportion of objects in the later of the two records that were also present in the earlier record. (Objects for which this comparison could not be made, because a subject had either not been present or rejected a Card on one of the two occasions, were excluded from this part of the analysis.)

The agreements between records adjacent in time (first at annual, later at longer intervals) were very low at early ages, being as low as 15% on average between the ages of 4 and 5. Agreement gradually increased over the years, with a trough at the age of 10, which coincided with the peak in the number of reported objects at this age. (In fact, the number of recurring objects was not greatly different at age 10, but the number of new objects was much higher than at other ages.) The greatest agreement was found between ages 18 and 35: 45% of objects, close to every second object, appearing in the records for age 35 had also been reported by the same subjects 17 years previously. There is little difference between the sexes: the girls' developmental trend was ahead of boys' at earlier ages, but this difference was statistically significant only for the interval of 6 to 7 years (p<.05, χ^2 = 4.052, DF = 1).

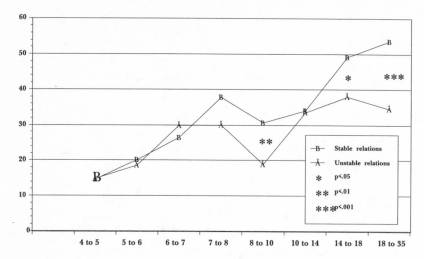

Figure 5. Year-to-year agreement of reported objects (%) for subjects with histories of stable and unstable relationships.

In terms of developmental stability, as can be seen from Figure 5, there is a clear difference between the group of subjects with a history of stable relationships and the group which had lived in unstable relationships.

The "stables" first showed a substantially higher year-to-year agreement of reporting at the age of eight. At the age of 35 as many as 54% of the objects in the records of the stables also appeared in their earlier adjacent records (at age 18); this figure was only 35% for the "unstables." Differences between the groups were significant at the age intervals 8 to 10 years (p<.01, χ^2 = 9.157, DF = 1), 14 to 18 years (p<.05, χ^2 = 3.884, DF = 1) and 18 to 35 years (p<.001, χ^2=14.451, DF = 1).

Discussion

In the present study, differences in recurrence rates were found both between different classes of objects and between groups of subjects with divergent histories in terms of relationship stability.

It should be pointed out that two extreme groups were selected from a representative sample; and also that, since there was no comparison or reference group, the results cannot be generalized to a normal population. Moreover, it must be borne in mind that, when comparing the relative frequencies of different categories of objects, the age of the sub-

166

jects at the time of the reports was not taken into account. Since the series covers childhood, adolescence and part of adulthood, it is not possible to generalize these findings to populations of any specific age. It may be that some of the effects reported are present for only a certain age period.

It is interesting to speculate over the reasons for the group difference between "stables" and "unstables" found in the present study. It might be hypothesized, as we have already suggested, that subjects with a history of relatively stable, and less unhappy, relationships have greater access to their feelings and memories, and less need for defensive operations in dealing with the outside world. It could also be argued that persons with relatively little stability in their lives are forced to develop more quickly or make more drastic personal changes, with the consequence that there is greater change in their personalities over the life course. Other explanations include the possibilities that persons with stable (and perhaps conventional) lives become more conventional in their cognitive mediation, or that "unstables" put less effort into information processing than "stables." Which is the most plausible interpretation cannot be determined from the data presented in the present study. However, it is possible to test all these hypotheses using data available within the Solna study, and we hope to be able to carry out such investigations in the future.

Understanding the nature of the phenomenon of the recurrence of objects in the Rorschach requires several factors to be taken into consideration. A response may recur for one of many reasons. First, there is the chance effect, or to be more precise, the "chance-like" production of similar responses to the blots due to their actual features.

A second obvious reason for recurrences is that the basic psychological styles or tendencies that are reflected in Rorschach responses are expected to have some temporal stability; thus, the same response may be selected in a retest situation, through the same mechanisms that operated on the first occasion.

A third reason for recurrence is that the subject remembers his or her impressions of the blots, or the actual responses he or she had delivered on earlier test occasions. Higher or lower recurrence rates for different classes of objects have been interpreted above in terms of how easily memories of the objects would form. It has been hypothesized that such memory formation is less likely to take place when relatively poor information processing or some types of defensive operations or projection is involved in the response process. On this view, memories are more

167

likely to form when the subject is putting energy into information processing and cognitive mediation. It is also possible, of course, that some contents (e. g., human figures) are more easily remembered *per se*.

To be able to speak of a "memory effect," however, it is not enough that the subject simply remembers his or her earlier responses. In the response process, the subject must also choose to deliver the remembered response, rather than other possible responses. Only then is the delivered response different from what it would have been on a first test occasion. This would be the case, for example, if an individual adopted a "memory strategy" as a defense; that is, if he or she remembered and reported the same objects over and over again in order to avoid having to deal with new impressions of the blots.

In an individual retest, the three effects (chance, stability of personality and memory) are altogether inseparable, but in groups studied over time, it is possible to separate out at least parts of the different effects.

The expected impact of the chance effect could be estimated from normative material. Alternatively, it could be separated from other phenomena in a test-retest study, using comparisons between the t_1 records of subjects and the t_2 records of other, unrelated subjects to obtain the "chance" rate of recurrence.

It is more difficult to separate personality and memory effects. Nevertheless, one way to estimate the effect of memory would be to compare the latest records in a longitudinal series to the first records of subjects from a comparable group.

If some individuals adopt a "memory strategy" to avoid involvement in the test material, this might be expected to be reflected in other tests and projective materials. Thus, if the same individuals have recurring response behaviors in other materials, this could be taken as evidence of a memory effect, or the adoption of a memory strategy. Within the framework of the Solna study, numerous personality investigation methods have been used repeatedly, and it is certainly possible to test this hypothesis.

It should be said that even if a memory effect can be demonstrated for the recurrence of objects, its impact on the stability of other Rorschach variables is unclear. Other research (Exner, Armbruster, & Viglione, 1978) has shown core Rorschach variables to remain stable while the recurrence of responses is being manipulated experimentally.

In our future work in this area, we shall include the total study group, and extend the analysis to other Rorschach data in addition to those used in the present study.

168

Résumé

L'étude que nous présentons porte sur la répétition des contenus de réponses Rorschach dans les données longitudinales recueillies pendant une trentaine d'années. On a sélectionné 20 sujets dans un groupe de 212 participants à une étude développementale prospective. Ceuxci ont été testé neuf fois entre 4 et 35 ans. On a opéré la sélection de telle sorte qu'il y ait autant d'hommes que de femmes, et autant de sujets présentant une histoire relationnelle stable qu'instable.

On a comparé la fréquence de répétition de certaines classes d'objets. On a trouvé qu'il y avait un taux relativement élevé de répétition des réponses banales, des objets ayant une qualité formelle ordinaire, des objets localisés en W ou en D, des objets humains et animaux, et des objets habituellement perçus en rapport avec un objet animé. On a trouvé des taux de répétition assez bas pour les objets ayant une qualité formelle inhabituelle (u) ou moins, ceux localisés en Dd, et ceux qui correspondent aux contenus Anatomie, Art, Alimentation (Fd) et Science.

Les sujets qui avaient vécu des relations stables présentaient plus de stabilitée dans leurs protocoles que les autres. Quelques hypothèses explicatives sont proposées. Enfin, la nature du phénomène de répétition est discutée en relation avec trois facteurs qui sont le hasard, la stabilité de la personnalité et la mémoire.

Resumen

Este estudio se ocupa de la recurrencia de objetos reportados en los protocolos de Rorschach, en datos recolectados en una investigación longitudinal a lo largo de aproximadamente treinta años. Veinte sujectos fueron seleccionados a partir de un grupo de 212 participantes en en studio prospectivo del desarrollo, a los cuales se las había administrado el Rorschach en 9 ocasiones entre los 4 y los 35 años de edad. Los casos fueron seleccionados de manera de proveer una cantidad equivalente de sujetos masculinos y femeninos, y con historias estables e inestables en cuanto a las relaciones interpersonales.

Se compararon las proporciones relativas de recurrencia para diferentes clases de objectos reportados. Se encontró que hubo una proporción relativamente alta de recurrencia para las respuestas Populares, objetos con un nivel de Calidad Formal Ordinaria, objectos localizados en las áreas *W* o *D,* objetos con contenido Humano y Animal, y objectos reportados comunmente en conjunción con un objeto viviente. Se encontraron proporciones relativamente bajas de recurrencia para objetos con Calidad Formal Inusual o Negativa, objetos localizados en áreas *Dd,* y objetos en las categorias de Contenido de Anatomia, Arte, Comida y Ciencia.

Se encontró que los sujetos que habían vivido relaciones estables mostraron una mayor estabilidad en sus protocolos de Rorschach que aquellos que habían vivido relaciones inestables. Se discuten las razones posibles de esta diferencia. Finalmente, se discute la naturaleze del fenómeno de la recurrencia en términos de tres efectos: azar, estabilidad de la personalidad y memoria.

References

Dagberg, K., Houdi, A., & Stattin, H. (1991). *The Use of Projective Techniques in Longitudinal Research: Relating Early Rorschach Ratings of Children to Their Later Criminal Behavior.* Paper presented at the European Science Foundation Conference on Longitudinal Research, Budapest (Hungary), March 1991.

Exner, J. E. (1980). But it's only an inkblot. *Journal of Personality Assessment, 44,* 563–576.

Exner, J. E. (1986). *The Rorschach: A Comprehensive System. Volume I: Basic foundations* (2nd ed.). New York: Wiley.

Exner, J. E. (1990). *A Workbook for the Comprehensive System.* Asheville, North Carolina: Rorschach Workshops.

Exner, J. E. (1991). *The Rorschach: A Comprehensive System. Volume II: Interpretation* (2nd ed.). New York: Wiley.

Exner, J. E., Armbruster, G. L., & Viglione, D. (1978). The temporal stability of some Rorschach features. *Journal of Personality Assessment, 42,* 474–482.

Karlberg, P., Klackenberg, G., Engström, I., Klackenberg-Larsson, I., Lichtenstein, H., Stensson, J., & Svennberg, I. (1968). The development of children in a Swedish urban community. A prospective, longitudinal study. *Acta Paediatrica Scandinavica, 187 (Suppl.).*

Klackenberg-Larsson, I. (1980). *Rorschachtestet 4-8 år.* Stockholm: Kliniken för Studium av Barns Utveckling och Hälsa, Karolinska Sjukhuset. (Mimeographed report.)